Mat Time 2
More Devotions to Enrich Your Martial Arts Classes

By: Ginny Tyler

ISBN: 978-1-7336151-2-9

Glory to God, who is able to do far beyond all that we could ask or imagine by his power at work within us.

Ephesians 3:20

Day 1: Spiritual Traps

Key verse(s): Galatians 5:1
"It is for freedom that Christ has set us free. Stand firm then, and do not let yourselves be burdened again by the yoke of slavery."

How many of you have had the uncomfortable predicament of sparring someone who simply stands in front of you, perfectly relaxed, with their hands at their sides?

You may have wondered why they didn't have their hands up. Maybe you were curious why they didn't come after you right away (and perhaps that made you nervous as well). You might have even thought to yourself, "why don't they do something already?" as you tried to decide whether to hold your ground or move in to attack.

Eventually you decided to close the gap and go towards them, hoping you weren't walking into a trap when BAM! What just happened?? Before you could get one hand technique in, you had five or six come flying at you from your opponent, and you wondered how someone could possibly be so fast.

My friends, you just walked into a trap.

Let's take another look at today's key verse. "Stand firm, then, and do not let yourselves be burdened again by the yolk of slavery." Now, it is important to note that I used the NIV version, which tends to be easier to understand. In the original King James translation, however, the wording is a bit different. Rather than saying "do not let yourselves be burdened again by the yoke of slavery", the King James version says, "be not entangled again with the yoke of bondage."

When you take into account that sentence structure was different back then, this verse would have sounded more like: "And not again in a yoke of slavery entangle yourselves." Did you catch that? This paints a rather different picture. The original version of this verse puts the responsibility of the ensnared person on themselves for walking into the trap, not on the trap itself.

In life, we often find ourselves in predicaments that we did not see coming, and rarely do we examine our own lives to see if there was something we could have done to avoid that trap in the first place.

Does anyone know what a commonly used trap is called? I'll give you a hint: the Bible mentions this word many times from cover to cover. It is called a snare.

What's interesting about a snare is that it is typically a loop on the ground that seems harmless to anyone who may see it (if they even see it), but once something walks through it, their own forward movement catches the snare and causes it to tighten until it eventually traps them. This concept really brings to light the fact that when we are trapped by sin or bad circumstances, we fail to see the many times we could have repented and turned away before we were hopelessly in bondage to it.

My challenge to all of you this week is to examine your lives and see what snares may be laid for you in the life choices you make, the people you surround yourselves with, and your spiritual discernment regarding what you allow into your life in the way of entertainment. Maybe you see a snare on the road ahead, or perhaps there is even one on your leg right now. If so, now is the time to loosen it before you are bound and trapped for good.

Use the space below to add your thoughts, experiences, and convictions to make this message more personal for your audience.

Day 2: Keep Moving

Key verse(s): Numbers 14:3-4
"…'Why is the Lord bringing us to this land only to let us fall by the sword? Our wives and children will be taken as plunder. Wouldn't it be better for us to go back to Egypt?' And they said to each other, "We should choose a leader and go back to Egypt.""

Raise your hand if you enjoy staying in the same rank for a long time. There are definitely some benefits, right? You know all of your material very well, and because of that, you tend to stand out from those that just ranked up not too long ago. You may have mastered the skills you needed to learn in that rank, and you generally feel good about working out in class. Then, like clockwork, just when you seem to be in a good place in your current rank, it's test time, you earn a new rank, and it's almost like being a new student all over again as you learn more kata(s), self-defense, one-steps, and more. You may be eager to learn all of the new material, but perhaps you don't feel as confident in class as you did before that test.

In today's passage, the Israelites were uncomfortable with the idea of moving into the promised land. They let their fears get the best of them, and rather than having faith in God's providence, they actually wanted to go back to their bondage in Egypt – simply because it was what was familiar to them. I don't know about you, but I can't imagine seeing all of the miracles God did for them as they left Egypt and wandered the desert, and yet they still wanted to go back to what they were delivered from.

This is especially ironic because the Israelites had a wine-making tradition that would have struck home in this scenario: Wine was never left in the same pot for too long of a period. You see, it had to be moved from time to time, because if it was left in the same pot, bacteria and contaminants would sink to the bottom, multiply, and taint the entire batch. By moving the wine from pot to pot every so often, the cleaner wine near the top would move into a fresh pot, but the yucky stuff would stay in the original pot. Overall, the process kept their entire batch cleaner, safer, and much better tasting.

Now, backtrack for a minute. If wine will go bad when left stagnant for too long, why would the Israelites want to go *back* to their original prison?

What we don't always realize is that God keeps us on our toes so that we, too, can grow and not become impure or fall into the same traps of sin that, though wrong, may be comfortable to us.

A famous quote by Gichin Funakoshi, the father of Shotokan karate, reads, "To stand still is to regress." Students, this is very much the case if you do not continue to move forward, learn new things, and challenge yourself.

This week, I would like for you all to look for an area where you tend to stick to your comfort zone and push yourself outside those boundaries a bit. Let's see what God has for you on the other side!

Use the space below to add your thoughts, experiences, and convictions to make this message more personal for your audience.

Day 3: Taking Your Prayer Life to the Next Level

Key verse(s): Matthew 6:9-13
"'This, then, is how you should pray: Our Father in heaven, hallowed by your name, your kingdom come, your will be done, on earth as it is in heaven. Give us today our daily bread. And forgive us our debts, as we also have forgiven our debtors. And lead us not into temptation, but deliver us from the evil one.'"

When we have class, we typically cover the same facets of training in each class, with some variation thrown in here and there for fun. We practice katas, hand and foot techniques, self-defense, sparring, one-steps, and character building. This structure is to ensure that our classes are well-rounded and cover more ground.

Did you know that God wants our prayers to be the same? Today's key verse reminds us of what we need to strive to integrate into each of our prayers, and we will use the acronym ACTS to help us remember them:

Adoration – God spoke the world and everything in it into existence. He deserves our praise for His continued providence, grace, and love.

Confession – What do we need to do better? Rather than make excuses for our sin, we need to take responsibility for it and repent.

Thanksgiving – If you woke up this morning with breath in your lungs, if you had food on your table, if you are safe, and if you are loved, God deserves to be thanked. This list is definitely not inclusive of everything we should verbalize our gratitude for.

Supplication – Usually, this is the only regular aspect to a person's prayer life. We should not be praying just to ask for things, as this is the last of four facets of prayer. Also, remember to ask for your needs, but we don't need to ask for every little thing we want as well. Trust God to overflow your cup.

My challenge to everyone this week is to examine your typical prayers. Are you incorporating adoration, confession, thanksgiving, and supplication? If not, make yourself a note where you usually say your prayers to be sure and include all of the above. Remember, students, just like the breakdown of our classes, we should also have well-rounded prayers!

Use the space below to add your thoughts, experiences, and convictions to make this message more personal for your audience.

Day 4: Ambassadors in Training

Key Verse(s): 2 Corinthians 5:20
"We are therefore Christ's ambassadors, as though God were making his appeal through us. We implore you on Christ's behalf: Be reconciled to God."

Oftentimes, our karate school visits other schools for the goal of cross training via seminars, competing in tournaments, or even testing together. How do you think I would feel if you were disrespectful to the other instructors, running wild, or talking through someone else's test? *(Take this opportunity to praise your students if they have been exemplary in these situations.)*

Today's verse reminds us that when you go to these special events, you are acting as ambassadors of your karate school. Can any of you tell me exactly what an ambassador is?

An ambassador is someone who represents the interests of their home, organization, family, church, or in the most commonly used form of the definition, their country. So, who here is an ambassador?

What if I told you that you are always an ambassador of Christ? Think about that for a moment. Students, we are representatives of the glory of God and our future home in Heaven while in this foreign land we call earth. How do you think God feels about the way we are conducting ourselves in our day-to-day lives? How do you think He feels about the life choices we make? We would be wise to always remember that through us, people will either see the love and power of God in our lives, or the lack thereof. And it is in those observations others make about how well we represent God that they may decide whether or not they want to give their lives to Christ.

This week, be mindful of the way you carry yourself. Do you have an attitude of pride or humility? Be mindful of the way you treat others. Are you treating them how you would like to be treated? Be slow to anger, quick to forgive, and take all opportunities you can to be at peace with and a blessing to everyone around you. You never know who may be watching.

Use the space below to add your thoughts, experiences, and convictions to make this message more personal for your audience.

Day 5: A Better View

Key Verse(s): Isaiah 55:8-9
"'For my thoughts are not your thoughts, neither are your ways my ways,' declares the Lord. 'As the heavens are higher than the earth, so are my ways higher than your ways and my thoughts than your thoughts.'"

Raise your hands if you have come to class feeling really good about your practice time during the week and thinking your kata or technique is just perfect. We bow in and begin working out, and you are so excited that this is your chance to show everyone just how flawless you look.

But once class took off, one of the instructors, or even I, had a list of corrections for you. Maybe your ready hand was not quite right. Or perhaps your kick could have been higher. You could have gotten your block folds mixed up, and by the end of class, you were frustrated that there was *still* so much to work on!

Today's key verses remind us that each of us has a picture in our head that is our own perspective. Unfortunately, as the student, many of your perspectives aren't as "high" as someone's who has trained in the martial arts for years. Someone who has more experience sees not only what you do in the present, but also how far you still need to go. Oftentimes, the vantage point of the instructor is to see what needs to be corrected before you are at their level, and unfortunately, it takes a fair amount of humility to acknowledge this in a way that doesn't leave you disappointed.

I'm sure you are all familiar with the story of Joseph, who was sold into slavery by his jealous brothers. At the time, Joseph likely had a very narrow perspective on what was happening, but when we read in the book of Genesis, chapter 39, we find that he was taken to Egypt and eventually put in charge of Potiphar's household. How his fortune changed! Did he know that would happen? Of course not. Did God? Absolutely.

As we go farther into the chapter, we see that Potiphar's wife tried to tempt Joseph into sin, but he refused to give in to it. To punish him for refusing her, Potiphar's wife lied about Joseph's intentions and had him put into prison for years. This must have been a really hard time for Joseph, because seemingly, he was being punished for doing what was right. Again, we see that he did not have a chance to see the bigger picture until later.

Fast forward to chapter 41 and we see that Joseph was trusted with a very important task. The Pharaoh wanted Joseph to interpret a dream for him, which, through the power of God, he was able to do. Because of this, not only was Joseph released from prison, but he was put in charge of all of Egypt just under Pharaoh himself!

The dream that Joseph interpreted spelled f-a-m-i-n-e for all of Egypt for a period of seven years, after seven years of plenty. Because of the wisdom given to him, Joseph was able to save the country from starvation, including neighboring communities and his own family that had sold him so many years prior.

What we have to remember is that when God sees our actions, thoughts, and choices, He knows what that final product should look like and how far we all still have to go to get there. Did Joseph get to see the big picture during the hard times? No. Did he have faith in God's plan nonetheless? Yes. In fact, this became one of the most famous "but God" testimonies in all of the Bible, and like all great stories, sometimes we just have to wait until the end to get a glimpse of the bigger picture that we didn't get to see in the beginning.

Use the space below to add your thoughts, experiences, and convictions to make this message more personal for your audience.

Day 6: It Comes Naturally

Key Verse(s): 1 Corinthians 9:25
"Everyone who competes in the games goes into strict training. They do it to get a crown that will not last, but we do it to get a crown that will last forever."

Do you all remember your first day at (*school name here*)? Maybe a couple of you did really well, but I would say the majority of all new students come to class a bit shaky, uncoordinated, and struggling with the balance necessary to do most of the things you learned adequately.

For the student that does really well from day one, it definitely gives them an advantage in class. They tend to move up in ranks quicker, look more confident, and maybe they don't have to practice quite as hard as the rest of the students. But does that mean they are *better* than the rest of the class?

Which type of student do you think I prefer to see? The one with natural talent or the one who has to work twice as hard to earn the same rank?

Today's key verse reminds us that it is not the perishable crown that is most important. That means, it is not the flashiest technique, the highest scoring student in a tournament, or even the one who can earn their black belt the fastest. All of those rewards are perishable, meaning they can fade and lose value. As we get older, your technique will slow down, the trophies will gather dust, and your belts may just be a decoration on your walls.

Matthew 6:19-21 reiterates this fact: "Do not store up for yourselves treasures on earth, where moths and vermin destroy, and where thieves break in and steal. But store up for yourselves treasures in heaven, where moths and vermin do not destroy, and where thieves do not break in and steal. For where your treasure is, there your heart will be also."

Natural talent can be a good thing, but more valuable to me is the student who comes to class with self-control, integrity, humility, patience, and a hard work ethic. Those are the things that will not fade or break over time. Those are the things that will only help you in other areas of your life. And perhaps, just perhaps, those are the things that would actually earn you a black belt sooner.

My challenge to all of you this week is to focus on the tenets of the martial arts. Remember the acronym CHIPSI:

Courtesy

Humility

Integrity

Perseverance

Self-Control

Indomitable Spirit

(add any additional you use in your classrooms)

If you feel that any of these tenets are lacking in your actions, focus on getting it/them up to speed.

Use the space below to add your thoughts, experiences, and convictions to make this message more personal for your audience.

Day 7: Hard Vs. Soft

Key Verse(s): 1 Corinthians 9:22
"To the weak I became weak, to win the weak. I have become all things to all people so that by all possible means I might save some."

Students, let's talk about hard and soft styles of martial arts. Hard styles focus on both defense and counter strikes via punches, kicks, and techniques that rely on physical power and force. Blocks can be emphasized, but they also serve as an attack as well. Some examples of a hard style of martial arts are karate, tae kwon do, and muay thai.

In soft styles, however, the emphasis is more on yielding, or using your opponent's force against them. Rather than trying to stop an attack altogether, the defender would move with it and manipulate the force to work against the attacker. Soft styles tend to focus on the "internal" over the "external". Some examples of soft styles include kung-fu, tai chi, and aikido.

Regardless of the type of martial art, each style has a benefit to the practitioner, including better focus and confidence, increased flexibility and physical strength, learned self-defense skills, better self-discipline, and more. All in all, there are many options to meet the same end goal.

In today's key verse, we read that Paul is utilizing flexibility in a different way to reach a broad audience with the Gospel. As he states, "I have become all things to all people so that by all possible means I might save some."

We all have different strengths and talents when it comes to sharing our faith. Perhaps you are more social and like to talk to others face to face. Or, you could be artistic and use your talents to share the gospel through your art. Are you a musician? You could bring others to Christ through your music. Maybe you have a heart to serve, and it is in doing so that you will reach others, either on your own turf or on the mission field.

Whatever route you take, it's the same end goal. Imagine having the capacity to change your approach based on the audience you have. Would that be hard for you? This week, try to stretch those boundaries a bit and see what comes of it!

Use the space below to add your thoughts, experiences, and convictions to make this message more personal for your audience.

Day 8: The Spotless Lamb

Key Verse(s): Luke 2:12
"This will be a sign to you: You will find a baby wrapped in cloths and lying in a manger."

When you all first got your uniforms, what color were they? *(Let students answer "white")* Take a look at them now. Are they still just as spotless? How about some of the other black belts you've seen – are their uniforms just as white? Probably not. Over time, those uniforms start to pick up dirt that may not come out in the wash, or they may get grass stains on them if you play outside after class. What about sweat stains? Or worse, blood!

The point is, as perfect as those uniforms start out, they never stay as pristine as the day you took them out of the package. Nothing in this world will be unmarred because of the unfortunate side effects of living in a fallen world. Our bodies may also accumulate scars, but more so, our souls will pick up spiritual dirt and decay as well.

But there is one who left this world just as spiritually perfect as He entered it: Jesus. In today's key verse we are reminded of what the angel Gabriel announced to the shepherds on the night of Jesus' birth. He was telling them where to find the baby, but more importantly, he was making a statement about the person they were to find. Indirectly, he was telling the shepherds that Jesus, the newborn baby, would always be the perfect, blemish-free sacrifice to save all of mankind.

You see, in Biblical times, it was a Jewish custom to set aside all of the first-born baby lambs to be holy and reserved for the Lord (aka, sacrificed during Passover) to atone for the sins of each family. Each family needed a spotless lamb, which totaled an estimated 250,000 lambs each year!

But there was a catch. Each lamb had to be blemish free in addition to being the first-born. So, after the birth of such a lamb, it was wrapped in swaddling cloths to signify their position as the potential sacrifice. They were then placed in a manger until they could be examined for physical defects or blemishes. If they met the criteria, they would be taken to

Jerusalem for the yearly feast.

So, the defining protocol for the sacrificial lambs was that they would be wrapped in cloths and placed in mangers until it was time for the priests to decide if they were an acceptable sacrifice. When Gabriel was telling the shepherds the condition in which they would find the newborn king, he was also indirectly saying that He would be the one who would atone for all of their sins as well.

The unfortunate nature of the sacrificial lamb was that despite being spotless, the yearly sacrifice was never enough to atone for *all* of the Jewish people's sins, including the ones they would commit in the future. But not so with Jesus. In John 19:30, just before He died, He said, "It is finished." His death on the cross put an end to the necessity for all sacrifice, for He truly *was* the perfect sacrifice.

The next time you throw those uniforms in the wash, let it be a reminder that there was one man who was and always will be purer than anything you will ever find on this earth.

Use the space below to add your thoughts, experiences, and convictions to make this message more personal for your audience.

Day 9: Resistance Training

Key Verse(s): James 1:2-3
"Consider it pure joy, my brothers and sisters, whenever you face trials of many kinds, because you know that the testing of your faith produces perseverance."

Raise your hands if you would like to do horse stances or back stances for ten minutes or more each week in class? How about a cat stance? Is anyone up for the challenge? Why or why not? You may be asking, "Why do we even work on stances so much, anyway?" It seems like we practice them every class!

When we are practicing stances, it is a form of resistance training. You see, we are resisting gravity and our own weight, and by doing so, we get stronger each time. You may be sore the next day or two, but that pain is actually part of a necessary process to gain strength. When your muscles hurt, it is because they get microscopic tears in them while working out. But as your muscles heal those tears, they also grow, resulting in more muscle mass and stamina for your next workout. The age-old adage "No pain, no gain" is aptly stated.

Similarly, we can also have spiritual resistance training, where we go through seasons of pain, hurt, temptation, anger, and more, but as we heal and test our faith for those impurities, we invariably grow stronger. Then when the next "season" comes around, we will be more impervious to it as we navigate what comes with a stronger grasp on what it takes to stay afloat spiritually.

All of you are here for a reason. Perhaps it is to gain coordination and strength. Maybe you wanted to learn practical self-defense or enjoy the mind/body connection the martial arts have to offer. Whatever the reason, if you are investing the time into growing your physical muscles, you need to be doing the same for your spiritual muscles as well. The tests of faith are inevitable; be prepared.

Use the space below to add your thoughts, experiences, and convictions to make this message more personal for your audience.

Day 10: Crank up the Heat

Key Verse(s): Genesis 3:1
"Now the serpent was more crafty than any of the wild animals the Lord God had made. He said to the woman, 'Did God really say, "You must not eat from any tree in the garden?"'"

How would you all feel if I put you through a blue belt test after just a few weeks of karate training? How would you feel about being expected to perform as an advanced student when you only had a small amount of training? How would you feel if I expected you to complete a black belt test after just a month of classes?

The truth is that none of you would be able to pass either of those tests, but why is that? Because to adequately train for any physical test, it takes time. You can't expedite the process of going from a beginner to an advanced rank, and I wouldn't expect you to because it's just not possible. You would have to build up your skills, coordination, and strength slowly so that you could get used to all of the requirements before moving on to your next challenges.

In today's verse, we see just how clever the serpent was in the Garden of Eden. He knew that if he told Eve outright to eat the apple that she likely wouldn't do it. It's easy to see a sinful choice when it is right in front of our faces, isn't it?

Rather than risk losing this battle, Satan took the slower (and more effective) approach. First, he planted a seed of doubt in Eve's mind by questioning what God had told her regarding eating the forbidden fruit. Next, he outwardly contradicted God's command when Eve misinterpreted His word by telling her that she would *not* die if she ate the fruit. (Spoiler alert: he knew that she would assume a quick physical death, and he was banking on that assumption) Lastly, he tempted her via her pride. Eating fruit that would make her as wise as God? I'm sure that Eve was imagining all she could do with that knowledge, assuming the fruit would not kill her, after all.

So rather than get straight to the point with the sinful temptation, Satan took a more subtle approach to make her want to try that fruit so badly that she would not see it as wrong. Isn't that the way most mistakes happen, students?

Maybe if someone came right out and told you to cheat on your test, you would say no right away. But if you are having trouble on test day, and someone just happens to slide their paper to the edge of their desk so you could see it, it might not seem as wrong if you are just sneaking one quick peek.

What if you see someone drop money out of their pocket, and you grab it quickly to return it to them. But then you see that new video game in the showcase window of the store right next door. Is it really wrong to keep that money? After all, they did drop it, and that may not seem the same as stealing. (But it is.)

It's up to all of us to recognize that sin is still sin, even if it creeps into your life slowly and tries to desensitize us to the reality that it is wrong. We must train ourselves in discernment to stop sinful habits and thoughts right away before the line between right and wrong is blurred. The enemy has been playing that card from the very beginning, and we need to be acutely aware of that and try to break the cycle of sin.

If you are struggling with discerning right from wrong in a particular are of your life, I challenge you to speak with your parents and pray about it this week.

Use the space below to add your thoughts, experiences, and convictions to make this message more personal for your audience.

_____

_____

_____

_____

_____

_____

_____

_____

_____

_____

_____

_____

_____

_____

Day 11: Obedience is Gold

Key verse(s): 1 Samuel 15:22
"But Samuel replied: 'Does the Lord delight in burnt offerings and sacrifices as much as in obeying the Lord? To obey is better than sacrifice, and to heed is better than the fat of rams.'"

Students, how do you think I would feel if you came to class each week with a gift in your hands for me? It might be an apple one week, or a handmade card another. Sentiments like that always make someone feel appreciated, don't they? Now, what if you were to do the same thing each week, but during class you would act up. Perhaps you would disobey commands, or talk out of turn. One day you might whine about all the work you had to do, or during mat time you may be disruptive. How do you think I would feel about your little gifts then? I would be thinking, "forget the gifts, just follow the class rules!"

You see, gifts don't matter if you have a heart of disobedience or disrespect. Gifting someone under those circumstances is what Jesus refers to as "whitewashed tombs" in Matthew 23:27. As he says, "Woe to you, teachers of the law and Pharisees, you hypocrites! You are like whitewashed tombs, which look beautiful on the outside but on the inside are full of the bones of the dead and everything unclean." Furthermore, if we backtrack to verse 26, Jesus also states, "Blind Pharisee! First clean the inside of the cup and dish, and then the outside also will be clean." As you can see, God believes that a healthy dose of introspection should come before an outward action.

If we look in 1 Samuel 15, we see the backstory to our key verse today. King Saul was leading an attack on the Amalekites and was instructed to destroy the city and everything in it. Unfortunately, he decided to keep the king as a hostage and spare the best of the animals, which spurred the prophet Samuel to ask him why he had disobeyed the Lord's orders. Saul answered that he had planned to sacrifice all of the animals to the Lord, to which Samuel countered with today's verse. Unfortunately, this was not Saul's only act of disobedience, and this last instance was the final nail in his proverbial coffin as king over the Israelites. Though he begged Samuel for forgiveness, he was then informed that the Lord would tear away his kingdom (and that He regretted giving him that position in the first place).

The lesson in all of this is that we should be searching our hearts and seeking to please the Lord in the ways that honor Him most. Gifts of the earth come second to the harder task of refining ourselves on the inside and submitting to His authority and instruction.

Use the space below to add your thoughts, experiences, and convictions to make this message more personal for your audience.

_____

_____

_____

_____

_____

_____

_____

_____

_____

_____

_____

_____

_____

_____

Day 12: Don't Look Back

Key Verse(s): Proverbs 26:11
"As a dog returns to its vomit, so fools repeat their folly."

Students, how many times have I corrected a technique of yours, only to have to remind you time and time again of the same thing before I see a change in habit? Raise your hand if I routinely correct your ready hand? How about those stances? Sometimes I feel like a broken record with the same reminders about "railroad tracks" and the back foot facing forward in your front stances. Have I corrected anyone's guard hands while sparring recently?

For most of you, you know that these techniques need to be changed, yet you seem to fall back into old habits just as quickly as the thought crosses your mind that you should be fixing it.

None of us are perfect, as you all know. And I certainly do not expect perfection. But what's important to understand here is the negative pattern of falling back into bad habits when you know better. Did you know the same thing happens in regards to our sinful habits? We know we should do better, but for a myriad of reasons, we can't quite seem to break that habit.

Today's key verse reminds us that when we return to sin but know better, it is like a dog returning to its… vomit. That's pretty gross, isn't it? Do any of you have dogs? Have you ever seen your dog do that? If only we felt the same disgust about ourselves returning to our own sin!

There are many traps laid for us in this world that primarily come from three places: the world itself, ourselves, and Satan. We try our best to overcome these temptations, but we have a continuous war going on inside of us. As Paul says in Galatians 5:17: "For the flesh desires what is contrary to the Spirit, and the Spirit what is contrary to the flesh." It's a never-ending war raging underneath our skin.

The good news is that Jesus is always willing to help us break free of those bad habits. His strength is all we need to overcome the shackles that bind our feet and hold us in a place of sin. All you need to do is ask for His help.

Use the space below to add your thoughts, experiences, and convictions to make this message more personal for your audience.

Day 13: The Martial Way

Key Verse(s): Revelation 3:16
"So, because you are lukewarm – neither hot nor cold – I am about to spit you out of my mouth."

Does anyone know what the Japanese term "budo" means? I'll give you a hint, the "do" portion is the same as in Tae Kwon Do. *(Allow students to try to answer)*

As I have mentioned before in class, "do" means "the way", and that just leaves us with the "bu", which means martial. So budo means the martial way, or having a way of life where the martial arts is an ongoing, integral part of it. It is letting this martial way of life transform the way you live, from the habits you form to the way you interact with the world around you.

This is opposed to the term jutsu, which refers to only the physical training aspect of a martial art. The physical results are the primary benefit you will see from this approach.

On one side, the martial art *is* your life, affecting the way you see the world around you and the way you treat those around you, and on the other, it is a small aspect of your life that involves physical training but does not typically incorporate any of the mind or spirit aspects.

As with anything in life, you can get as little or as much out of the martial arts as you want. But when you apply the same principle to your spiritual life, you get a very different picture. You see, you can live your life as a Christian and make it your "do". In this case, the fruit of the spirit would grow, positively affecting every portion of the way you handle life around you. Or you could treat your faith like the "jutsu" and be content with an hour at church each week, leaving your Bible on the bookcase as soon as you get home.

The problem with the latter is that God refers to this type of Christianity as "lukewarm". Neither hot, nor cold, and as such, useless to either end. Who likes a cup of hot cocoa? How about a chocolate milkshake? Both sound good, don't they? But who likes to make hot chocolate, set it on the table for an hour or so, and then drink it? Not very many people. God feels exactly the same about us when we are lukewarm.

If we are going to be hot, be HOT! Let your faith seep into every area of your life and see how it affects your joy, quality of life, and hope. If you choose to be cold, be cold. But to be lukewarm is to be neither here nor there, which even God Himself deems worthy of no better than being spit out.

Choose wisely, students, but in the words of Joshua in chapter 24, verse 15: "But if serving the Lord seems undesirable to you, then choose for yourselves this day whom you will serve, whether the gods your ancestors served beyond the Euphrates, or the gods of the Amorites, in whose land you are living. But as for me and my household, we will serve the Lord."

Use the space below to add your thoughts, experiences, and convictions to make this message more personal for your audience.

Day 14: What's Your Bunkai?

Key Verse(s): 1 John 2:6
"Whoever claims to live in him must live as Jesus did."

Does anyone know what the term "bunkai" means? In short, it means the practical application of your kata. When we do the first two steps of *(name one of your katas here)*, what exactly are you doing in those moves? *(Allow students to answer)* How about the next kata up? What is the practical application, or bunkai of the first two steps of *(name another kata)*?

It is imperative that we understand the bunkai of all of our katas, because if we didn't, what benefit are they to us? Are we just going through the motions and not considering why we are doing what we are doing? If we are going to put the work in, don't we want to reap all of the rewards for what we are learning? (Not to mention, that knowledge could save our lives one day!)

Thinking in terms of bunkai, what does that look like in our Christian life? How are we applying the principles of what we learn as Christians to our everyday life? In our key verse above, we are told that if we choose to follow Christ in faith, we are to live our lives as Jesus did. What does that look like to each of you? *(Allow students to answer)*

The Bible tells us so many amazing things about Jesus' character, and we would be wise to remember them all. Some of the first ones that come to my mind are the following:

- He put God first in every situation, even above his own comfort and needs. He also glorified God in all that He did, rather than keep any glory for Himself.

- He had immense compassion for those in need, those who were hurt, and those who were lost. He gave up His life to save people who had no problem mocking Him, beating Him, and rejecting Him. In fact, His response to this abuse is recorded in Luke 23:34 where He said, "Father, forgive them, for they do not know what they are doing."

- He had a fierce love for the church and hated to see it misused. In Matthew 21:12, we read: "Jesus entered the temple courts and drove out all who were buying and selling there. He overturned the tables of the money changers and the benches of those selling doves."

- Jesus never sought the approval of the crowds, nor did he take the popular route in life. He was never afraid to stand alone for His beliefs.

There are so many more aspects of Jesus' life that we are called to model, and I encourage each of you to search the Scriptures this week to learn more about how we are to do the same.

Use the space below to add your thoughts, experiences, and convictions to make this message more personal for your audience.

Day 15: Spiritual Dormancy

Key Verse(s): Exodus 20:8
"Remember the Sabbath day by keeping it holy."

Students, have you ever had a season where you just didn't want to come to class? Perhaps you were tired of doing the same techniques each week, or you might have been tired of working towards that next rank test. You see, beginner students get to test more often, but the higher in rank you go, the longer you have to wait. Is waiting a difficult thing? Does it get tedious or tempt you to just go through the motions in class? I know there are times when I see each of you practicing without zeal or excitement, and I also know exactly how that feels because I've gone through those same seasons when I was younger.

What are you doing in those seasons of repetition and waiting? Are you asking yourself how you can improve *while* you are waiting, or are you just letting that sour attitude get the best of you? What are you doing to better yourself *inside*?

The very same problem can be applied to our spiritual lives as well. Sometimes you feel as if you are walking through a spiritual desert. You may not feel as if you are growing, you don't feel like praying, you don't want to invest the time into reading the Bible, and perhaps you may have doubts about your salvation. What's important to remember when going through these seasons of spiritual dormancy is that our feelings are *not* authoritative. God's Word is true regardless of how we feel, and it is up to us to make the most of that time of rest.

Dormancy is a funny thing. Typically used when referring to plants and trees, the word implies that nothing is happening behind the scenes when, in fact, there is so much more going on than you can imagine. During dormancy, plants are not actively growing, but they are developing cold resistance for the coming winter. They are also carrying out many processes including respiration, photosynthesis, cell division, and enzyme production. This period of "rest" enables them to thrive when it is time to break dormancy and begin a time of new growth and fruitfulness.

Here's a fun fact: Did you know that most fruit trees *require* dormancy to take place, or else they won't produce fruit the next year? Who likes cherries, plums, or apples? We wouldn't have any of those fruits if they did not get enough chill hours to initiate a period of dormancy in the winter.

So you see, times of rest are required for us to be fruitful in the long run. In our key verse today, we see that God's fourth commandment says to keep holy the Sabbath day. This is not a time out for us! God knows that we need periodic times of rest and reflection so that we can have healthy growth afterwards.

Rather than let that time of "still" get you down, allow it to teach you something about yourself that will make you more fruitful in the long run.

Use the space below to add your thoughts, experiences, and convictions to make this message more personal for your audience.

Day 16: Be the Change

Key Verse(s): Mark 2:4-5
"Since they could not get him to Jesus because of the crowd, they made an opening in the roof above Jesus by digging through it and then lowered the mat the man was lying on. When Jesus saw their faith, he said to the paralyzed man, 'Son, your sins are forgiven.'"

I have seen many different personality types come through our doors over the years, and though the vast majority of my students have made me incredibly proud, many have made me feel very disappointed. You see, teaching the martial arts helps me to see the best and the worst in people at times, and it's hard to come to terms with some of the ones that I know have missed out on an amazing opportunity to better themselves, not just physically, but also emotionally and spiritually.

In today's key verses, we see a story about Jesus healing a paralyzed man in Capernaum. This man was bed-ridden, so his friends were carrying him over to see Jesus in hopes of a miracle. Upon arrival of the house Jesus was visiting, they saw that the crowds were going to make it impossible for them to get through to ask for this miracle. So instead of giving up, they made an opening in the roof and lowered their friend down into the house. Jesus saw the strength of their faith and healed the man.

No doubt, there were many different personality types in the crowded house that day, but I want to bring your attention to four of them:

- The Pharisees: These were people that were very well-versed in God's law, but despite that were spiritually dead. They lived lives of comfort and were respected by the masses, but they were egotistical, critical, and more interested in being right than in seeing the truth.

- The Crowds: Most of the people crowding the house were there for a good show, but likely lacking in true faith. They didn't come to Jesus because they believed in Him, but instead they were just hoping to see something spectacular happen. This same group was callous to the men trying to get their paralyzed friend in, and it's important to note that they were physically preventing the men from getting in the house.

- The Four Friends: So desperate for their friend's healing, they risked their own safety and comfort to bring their friend to Jesus. They were loyal, hopeful, and perseverant. They also physically carried their friend to Jesus, which has a deeper meaning than it seems at first glance.

- The paralyzed man: He was physically crippled but spiritually alive. His story became a miracle and brought hope to people all over the world for thousands of years. God used this man in a mighty way for His glory.

My question to all of you is, if given the choice, which character would you be? Your answer may just surprise you.

Use the space below to add your thoughts, experiences, and convictions to make this message more personal for your audience.

Day 17: Wheat and Tares

Key Verse(s): Matthew 13:24-26
"Jesus told them another parable: 'The kingdom of heaven is like a man who sowed good seed in his field. But while everyone was sleeping, his enemy came and sowed weeds among the wheat, and went away. When the wheat sprouted and formed heads, then the weeds also appeared. "

Have you students ever heard the expression, "a bad apple ruins the bunch?" What does that mean? *(Allow students to answer, then elaborate)*

Did you know that can be the same with people too? What if we had a student here that was a complete bully. By the way, I wouldn't allow that to happen, but let's just pretend. What if we had a student that was constantly too rough during sparring, they had a disrespectful attitude in class, and they bullied you before and after class. How would you feel about coming to train?

To anyone watching class; you could all look the same. Everyone would be wearing a white uniform with karate belts and would likely be doing the same exercises and kata, but for anyone who looked a little closer, they would know something wasn't quite right with the bully.

In today's key verses, Jesus is telling the parable of the wheat and tares. What are wheat and tares, and why are they important? Let me tell you a few things about wheat and tares, and then you can tell me if it sounds like the scenario I just described:

- Firstly, wheat and tares look nearly identical until harvest time (see below). So, it is incredibly hard to tell the difference between the two initially.

- Wheat is an edible grain that produces golden seeds for us to eat (nourishing). The seeds produce more of their own like kind (fruitful). The stems bow when they are mature and ready to harvest (humility). At that point, they are gathered for storage and use (gathered into the farmer's "house").

- Tares are inedible weeds that produce black seeds that are poisonous (usually causing nausea and vomiting). The seeds are infertile (not fruitful). The stems stay erect and stiff (pride). At this point, it's easy to tell which plants are the wheat, and which are the tares, since the wheat bows. But the problem with knowing this late is that the roots are intertwined together, and to try to remove the tares would only kill the wheat. Furthermore, the tares are gathered in bundles at harvest time to be burned.

Students, we live in a world full of both wheat and tares, and that is the reason I teach you how to fight both physical and spiritual battles. You also need to train yourself in discernment to be able to tell the difference before those tares are able to stop you from reaching fruitful maturity. When in doubt, look for the fruit of the Spirit in others. If you don't see any of that fruit, you need to be on your guard.

Use the space below to add your thoughts, experiences, and convictions to make this message more personal for your audience.

Day 18: Lean on Me

Key Verse(s): Galatians 6:2
"Carry each other's burdens, and in this way you will fulfill the law of Christ."

One of the perks of being a martial arts instructor is that I am always inspired when I see you reach your goals, grow as a martial artist, earn a new rank, and so much more. But one of my favorite things to see is when you all move through the ranks together and support your fellow classmates along the way. Even when you compete against one another at tournaments, I see you all encouraging each other, patting your friends on the back, or trying to cheer up those that didn't do as well as they had hoped. It is inspiring to see the way you band together and show me that you value the inner journey more than the immediate material goals.

Today's key verse reminds us that in our Christian walk, we are to do the very same thing. There are times when our brothers and sisters in Christ may be going through a hard season, feeling discouraged, or even making poor choices.

It's in those times that our Galatians 6:2 selves can really shine. They may need your encouragement, support, and/or prayers. Maybe you could go out of your way to remind them that God sees their hardship, and in doing so, they will see that they are not alone.

This situation is akin to a type of tree called a sequoia redwood, which is found in the California area. These trees are enormous! In fact, the tallest one is recorded at 275 feet tall! But in relation to their size above ground, the redwoods have relatively shallow roots supporting them. One would think that to have such a big, heavy tree with shallow roots, it would be a recipe for disaster. One big storm, and they could all come tumbling down!

But that is not the case, and I'll tell you why. Despite the shallow roots, these trees intertwine their roots with other redwoods, creating a network of support with one another so that they can withstand the storms and winds when they come. It's as if they are interlocking roots together just for the purpose of helping each other during times of trial, and because of it, they are all made stronger for it.

God's creativity never ceases to amaze me, as all of His creation brings glory to His name. Next time you know someone going through a hard time, remember those trees, helping brace each other for the storms, and aim to follow in their example. Remember, it only strengthens you too.

Use the space below to add your thoughts, experiences, and convictions to make this message more personal for your audience.

Day 19: Bought at a Price

Key Verse(s): 1 Corinthians 6:20
"...you were bought at a price."

Can some of you name me some of the equipment we use in our martial arts classes? (Allow students to answer) Some examples could include their own personal equipment: uniforms, sparring gear, belts, weapons and/or any training equipment they have at home. Examples at the dojo can include hand targets, kicking targets, stand up targets, re-breakable boards and more.

Did we get our equipment for free, or was it bought? What was it bought with? (*Allow students to answer*) So if we acknowledge that we bought all this equipment for a set amount of money, would you think that equipment is valuable or not? It is definitely worth taking care of, isn't it? If we are investing hard earned money into these things, we want to treat them with care and not neglect our investment, right?

For the next three weeks, we are going to be taking a deeper look at the most joyous of all Jewish customs: the Jewish wedding. This custom is a source of so many typological prophecies that it makes it well worth studying. The Jewish wedding is broken down into three parts:

- Preliminary Arrangements (Shiddukhin)
- Betrothal (Eyrusin)
- Marriage (Nissuin)

For the purpose of today's key verse, we will be studying the first part, the initial arrangements. This is the process by which the father of the groom (or another designated matchmaker) begins to look for a wife for his son so that they can move forward onto the next phase.

Once a suitable bride had been chosen, an agreement had to be made. The father of the bride would often stipulate a price for her dowry, and the bridegroom (or his family) would pay that price. (*Take a look at today's verse again*) Does this sound familiar?

Even though this was primarily prearranged, the bride's consent was usually taken into account as well. Once everyone was in agreement, the couple (and their families) would move onto the second phase of the marriage ceremony, which we will talk more about next week.

For today's talk, let's go back to our original discussion about the equipment. We decided that because we paid money for these things, they have value, correct? Yet in our key verse today, Paul is telling us we were all bought at a price as well. Were we bought for money? *(No)* What were we bought with? *(Allow students to answer)* We were bought with the life of Jesus, our Lord and Savior. If we deem things bought with money as valuable, how much more value do we have in Jesus' eyes for Him to give us His *life* for all of us?

I hope today's mat time reminds you of just how valuable you are in the eyes of God. Satan, the world, and even we sometimes devalue ourselves, but the God of the universe says you are all *priceless*. And it's His Word that matters most.

Use the space below to add your thoughts, experiences, and convictions to make this message more personal for your audience.

Day 20: Eternal Identity

Key Verse(s): John 10:28
"I give them eternal life, and they shall never perish; no one will snatch them out of my hand."

    Students, I have been training in the martial arts for (__) years, and throughout that time, I have seen how the arts have helped me physically, emotionally, and most of all, spiritually. There are so many lessons to be learned from your training, and contrary to what most people think, the more you learn, the more you realize *how much* there still is left to learn.

    Many students start the martial arts with great intentions (and some not), but the truth is that many more students begin the martial arts than those that actually earn the rank of black belt. Others quit the martial arts immediately after receiving that rank, thinking it's "the end of the line." If only they knew better! It really is a shame to invest so much time and hard work into something, only to leave it by the wayside as soon as you want to move onto something else.

    There is a Korean term "yeong-wonhan jeongcheseong", which means "eternal identity." This is the idea that you have made a personal decision to adopt something as a part of your identity – not merely invest in it for a short time or while the going is easy. You're in it for the long haul. That is what the martial arts mean to me. But even more so is my identity as a follower of Christ, which affects not just my earthly life, but also my eternal life.

    As people grow up, however, life happens, and with it comes the areas where we falter as we navigate living in a fallen world. We may begin to wonder if God still loves us when we make mistakes, and the enemy is right there, telling us that our sin is causing irreparable damage to our state of salvation. But as you can see in today's verse, Jesus is saying that no one can snatch us out of His hand. Not even ourselves.

    Last week, we touched on the three parts of a Jewish wedding custom. This week, we'll talk more about the second portion. In the betrothal phase of a marriage (Eyrusin), the couple holds a small, public ceremony to officially announce their intention to become engaged to each other. After the ceremony is over, for all legal purposes, the couple is married, but they do not live together quite yet. You see, the groom now has to build a home (or add a room onto his existing family home) to bring his new bride to later on. When the groom's father approves of the structure, he then gives permission for his son to get his bride. We will talk more about that next week.

What's important to remember is that during this period, only a legal divorce can separate these two people, and only the groom can initiate that divorce.

In the New Testament, Jesus is often referred to as "the bridegroom" who will one day return "for his bride" (aka the church). Taking the Jewish custom into account, we can see that only the "bridegroom" can divorce "the bride", and in today's verse, Jesus stated that no one will snatch the believers out of his hand. Isn't this a beautiful confirmation of Jesus' commitment to all of us?

I will leave you all with a question. Are you ready to commit your eternal identity to the One that honors us in such a way that He spared nothing to ensure that we would one day be able to dwell with Him in Heaven? Ultimately, it will be the most important decision you will ever make.

Use the space below to add your thoughts, experiences, and convictions to make this message more personal for your audience.

Day 21: The Big Day

Key Verse(s): Matthew 24:36
"But about that day or hour no one knows, not even the angels in heaven, nor the Son, but only the Father."

Let's start today's mat time with a question. How many of you practiced your karate this week? If today was a test day, how many of you *would have* practiced this week?

How come more of you raised your hands if there was an upcoming test? Shouldn't you be prepared, regardless of whether or not you have a test coming up?

Students, when you are a beginner or even intermediate, you often know exactly when your tests are, but by the time you get to an advanced rank with a time requirement of six months or more between tests, you often don't know when exactly your test day will be until it is almost upon you. So, wouldn't you think that it's better to be safe than sorry and practice even when you don't know you have an exam coming up? This week, we'll be talking about the third portion of the Jewish wedding custom: the marriage (Nissuin). Remember last week when I said the bridegroom couldn't come for his bride until his father gave him permission? Even being the son of the decision-maker, he still did not know when he would have that permission to go collect his bride.

Let's stop right there and connect that to our key verse today. *(Read it again)* This is another example of typological prophecy, showing us the relationship between the Old Testament and New Testament, specifically referring to Jesus' return.

When the father of the bridegroom gave permission for his son to go collect his bride, it was a joyous occasion that sometimes happened in the middle of the night! That's why the bride and her bridal party were to keep lamps burning each night as they anticipated the big day. Matthew 25:1 confirms this when Jesus says, "At that time the kingdom of heaven will be like ten virgins who took their lamps and went out to meet the bridegroom." He then goes on to say that the five that had not brought extra oil (were not prepared) were foolish, while the five that did bring extra oil (were prepared) were wise.

So my question to all of you is, what should we be doing while we wait for the return of Jesus?

From the bride's perspective, she had been preparing herself the past year (or more) spiritually for the upcoming wedding, waiting as patiently as possible. In addition, she had to prepare her garments for the upcoming wedding and spiritually cleanse herself for the new life to come.

So what should we all be doing while we wait? Are we to live a life that is fruitless, focused on earthly things, and focused only on ourselves? Or are we to spiritually prepare ourselves for the new life to come? Are we also supposed to be keeping "our garments clean" in preparation for the big day?

I will leave you all with just one more interesting nugget, and I'm sure many of you older students will be able to connect the dots. Once the bridegroom arrived at the house of the bride, his groomsmen were to lift her off her feet and physically carry her to the house the groom prepared (in his father's house), where the wedding was finalized, followed by a celebration that lasted seven days. (For my well-versed students, that's a period of seven). But once that wedding started, the gate doors were shut, and those who were not prepared would miss out on those seven days of festivities.

Students, I would encourage you to keep your lamps burning always. You never know when the party is going to start.

Use the space below to add your thoughts, experiences, and convictions to make this message more personal for your audience.

Day 22: Faith for All to See

Key Verse(s): Deuteronomy 6:9
"Write them on the doorframes of your houses and on your gates."

If I were to get a view of your front yards, or more specifically, your porches, what would that tell me about your beliefs, faith, or value?

If you have been to traditional Chinese restaurants or homes, you may have noticed that they often have statues outside their doors. In fact, in China, it is very common for people to have various statues, representing their faith and beliefs just outside their front doors. For example, have you ever seen the big lion statues of Chinese culture? There is typically a female on the left (to represent yin), as well as a male on the right (to represent yang). The belief is that the yin will protect the owners of the house, while the yang protects the structure of the house itself. There is also a commonly used Ch'an Chu statue, which is a three-legged toad that is said to protect the homeowner's wealth, as well as attract new riches. Has anyone seen a traditional dragon-turtle statue? To the Chinese, it is thought to bring success, strength, and courage to the owners. There are so many more examples, but as you can see, they are thought to bring (or retain) benefits to the owners' lives that would not be there if they did not own this idol.

The problem, however, is just that. They are idols, and they can be damaged, stolen, or worn with age. Most importantly, they don't have the power to do any of the things the people purchase them for, since they are created objects. Rather than worship the *creation*, we should strive to worship the *Creator*.

In our key verse today, we see that God wanted the Jewish people to portray their beliefs on the "doorframes of your houses and on your gates" for all to see before entering their homes. You see, the door or the gate is the place of entry to the home, and it is also the strongest point of protection. The custom of placing a m'zuzah (literally meaning "door frame") on the point of entry declares to everyone that your home is one dedicated to following God. But what exactly is a m'zuzah?

Simply put, it is a small box or fancy scroll holder that holds just that: a parchment with Biblical scripture on it (specifically Deuteronomy 6:4-9 and Deuteronomy 11:13-21). This statement of faith would be placed to the right of the doorway, either facing up and down, or tilted slightly towards the door on the top end.

When the Jewish people built or moved into a new home, the m'zuzah was one of the first things to go up. According to custom, it was legally required that it goes up no later than 30 days after moving into the new home, though most families would place it up much earlier than that.

Can anyone think of another instance in Old Testament times where the doorpost was used to show faith in God? Think back to the first Passover, when Moses instructed all of the Jewish people to paint lamb's blood on their door posts and lintels so that the angel of death would "pass over" the homes of the believers while striking down the first born of the Egyptians. The idea that the "blood of the lamb" saved them from death is yet another example of typological prophecy pointing God's chosen people to the coming Messiah.

As you can see, the idea of the entryway being a bold place to draw your line as a believer and find refuge inside from a fallen world is further supported in John 10:9, where Jesus states, "I am the gate; whoever enters through me will be saved."

My challenge for all of you this week is to take a look at the front door of your homes. Try to do something as a family to make a statement for the world to see about your faithfulness to the one, true God.

Use the space below to add your thoughts, experiences, and convictions to make this message more personal for your audience.

Day 23: Small World

Key Verse(s): Genesis 6:13
"So God said to Noah, "I am going to put an end to all people, for the earth is filled with violence because of them.""

All over the globe, different countries have their own styles of the martial arts, and often they have various styles even within their own political boundaries. China has kung fu, Japan has shotokan karate, Brazil has capoeira, Israel has krav maga, Okinawa has shorin ryu, Russia has systema, Korea has tae kwon do, and so many more! But they all have several things in common, regardless of their supposed origins.

Much in the same way, we find that despite their location on the globe, you will find similar accounts of Biblical events being passed down from generation to generation, regardless of which country you are in. Take the story of the great flood, for example. There are over 500 legends of this very same flood all over the world, including Greece, Egypt, India, the Pacific islands, and so many more. Though details may not all be exact, you will still find consistency in the idea that a man living in ancient times built a boat to save himself, his family, and animals from a great flood.

Even in countries that have a more secular approach to life have breadcrumbs in their history to back the story of a global flood. For example, the Chinese pictograph for boat consists of symbols for vessel + 8 + mouth (people). And we all know that Noah, his wife, and his 3 sons with their wives equals eight people. In addition, the pictograph for flood is made of symbols for water + total. Looking further, the symbol for total is made up of together + earth + eight. It is hard to see this as anything but the obvious: despite the pervasiveness and popularity of secular beliefs, the very basis for cultures around the world involve and confirm the word of God!

My challenge to all of you this week is to read through the story of Noah and the flood in Genesis, chapters six through eight. Next week, we will be talking more about why Noah and his family were chosen to be spared from the catastrophic flood, and I think the answer will surprise you all.

Use the space below to add your thoughts, experiences, and convictions to make this message more personal for your audience.

Day 24: Lost in Translation

Key Verse(s): Genesis 6:9
"This is the account of Noah and his family. Noah was a righteous man, blameless among the people of his time, and he walked faithfully with God."

Students, do you ever stop and think how amazing our bodies are and how creative God is to have so intentionally and perfectly designed us the way He did? I watch you all do your kicks, stances, blocks, self-defense, sparring, and more each week, and I still find it hard to fathom how intricate our bodies' blueprints are to be able to do so many marvelous things.

Even now, scientists are still discovering evidence of God's fingerprints all over His masterpiece that is called mankind. In Genesis 1:27, it says, "So God created mankind in his own image, in the image of God he created them; male and female he created them." But where is the signature in the bottom corner? After all, don't master artists leave their mark after they finish their work?

And so He did. I introduce to you laminin. Laminin is a protein present in all humans that has been referred to as the "glue" of the cells, keeping them in their proper place so that they can do their jobs correctly. Without laminin, we would not survive because nothing would be held together in its proper place. Colossians 1:17 says, "He is before all things, and in him all things hold together." This is aptly stated when you consider the chemical structure of laminin, which is shaped like a cross. Once again, science confirms what the Bible has already told us.

In today's key verse, we learn the reason Noah and his family were spared from the great flood. Genesis 6:9 states that he was "a righteous man, blameless among the people of his time...", and we need only to look at the other people of his time to confirm the difference.

Noah was living in a time when the fallen angels of Satan were tainting the DNA of mankind, creating a race of giants called the Nephilim. So widespread was this problem that every human on earth, save for Noah and his family, no longer had the same genetic code that God had created them to have.

They were corrupted and no longer able to be redeemed.

How do we know this? Look again at the word "blameless" in today's verse. The Hebrew translation of this word is tamim, which means blemish-free and physically pure. Remember when we talked about the Passover lambs that had to be blemish free and physically perfect? Tamim was also used to describe those that were without physical defects.

In essence, the fingerprints of God in the bodies of men were altered and no longer flawless compared to the way they were originally created. But because Noah and his family had uncorrupted DNA, they were chosen to be spared and begin new life again because they *still* bore the image of God.

This paints a very different picture than what we may have imagined, doesn't it? As you can see, we should not take lightly God's desire for us to keep our bodies pure and uncorrupted in all ways, especially genetically, for to fail to do so would imply that God has made a mistake. Satan is more than willing to tempt mankind with that forbidden fruit that we can fix God's original design, but I firmly believe that when God said "it was very good", it is not our place to question Him.

Use the space below to add your thoughts, experiences, and convictions to make this message more personal for your audience.

_____

_____

_____

_____

_____

_____

_____

_____

_____

_____

_____

_____

_____

_____

_____

_____

_____

_____

_____

Day 25: Unload

Key Verse(s): Ezekiel 36:25
"I will sprinkle clean water on you, and you will be clean; I will cleanse you from all your impurities and from all your idols."

Students, do you ever feel as if there is more to the action of putting on your uniform before class? Does it feel as if you are doing something significant before I call, "line up?"

I don't know about you, but when I put on my uniform before class, I imagine myself dropping the weight of the world as I prepare to begin. If there is something I am worried about, I let it go as I put my gi jacket on, and if I am holding onto anything else that would keep me from focusing on what I am about to do, I imagine it all going away as I tie my obi (belt). Furthermore, when I wear white, I am intentionally reminding myself to keep a humble spirit. If you think about it, there is a lot of emotional cleansing that goes on through the action of putting on your uniforms.

In our key verse today, we are reminded of the cleansing ritual of Baptism, though the custom dates back to Biblical times with a Jewish observance referred to as t'vilah, or ritual immersion. As you can see in today's key verse, Ezekiel referred to this custom as not only a physical cleansing, but also a spiritual one. Note where he says, "I will cleanse you from all your impurities and from all your idols."

The action of cleansing was meant to be so much more than just getting physical dirt off of your body. The primary intent of the custom was to provide a renewing of your mind through spiritual cleansing. We know this because oftentimes, Jewish people afflicted with a disease were told to cleanse *after* they were healed. In Luke 5:12-14, we see exactly this when Jesus was approached by a man with leprosy. Verse 13 states that, "immediately the leprosy left him", then in verse 14, Jesus instructs him to go to the priest to offer sacrifices for his cleansing.

In addition, we see a shift in the customs of t'vilah with John the Baptist, cousin of Jesus, who began baptizing people in the Jordan River as opposed to the traditional mikveh that was used by Jewish priests. You see, a mikveh was a special tub used by the priests in the temple for such ceremonies. For a man to be "offering the same service" in the river would have assuredly brought John the wrong type of attention from the priests who oftentimes profited from their services. John likely knew this was the case when they visited him in the wilderness (see Matthew 3:7).

All this to say, as with nearly all traditions established before Jesus was born, this one, too, was "rocked" with the physical coming of our Savior. In the words of Jesus Himself, "Do you see all these things? Truly I tell you, not one stone here will be left on another; every one will be thrown down." (Matthew 24:2) He was referencing the physical temple in Jerusalem, but as with everything He has said, there is a much deeper meaning than what first appears.

Use the space below to add your thoughts, experiences, and convictions to make this message more personal for your audience.

Day 26: Nice Shot

Key Verse(s): 1 Samuel 24:4
"This is the day the Lord spoke of when he said to you, 'I will give your enemy into your hands for you to deal with as you wish.' Then David crept up unnoticed and cut off a corner of Saul's robe."

Students, when we are sparring, it is very important to show respect to our partners, for they are helping us improve our technique. We bow to each other before each match, touch gloves, and bow when we are finished. But are we also acknowledging the times that they *could have* hit us but didn't? This can be as easy as a head nod at the time of the technique, or having a quick word with them when you are finished sparring. Regardless, it is important for us to communicate to our partner that we appreciate their self-control in *not* striking us when they could have.

Today's key verse is a small piece of a bigger story. You see, Saul had been pursuing (the soon to be) King David in the hopes of murdering him out of jealousy. Remember when we talked earlier about Samuel removing the blessing from King Saul? (We're beginning to see more to it than just his disobedience, aren't we?) That same blessing was placed on David (yes, the same David who defeated Goliath), and because of this, Saul was in a jealous rage and ruthlessly pursued David to kill him.

For years, David was on the run, until, in today's verse, we see that David and his followers were hiding in the very same cave that Saul went in to relieve himself. David could have killed Saul right then and there, but instead he decided to show him mercy because he was still technically the Lord's chosen king (first), and he was anointed so. Instead, David quietly cut off a corner of Saul's robe as a demonstration that he could have killed him but chose not to, then allowed him to leave.

Once Saul left the cave, however, David called out to him, bowed, and stated in verse 10: "This day you have seen with your own eyes how the Lord delivered you into my hands in the cave. Some urged me to kill you, but I spared you; I said, 'I will not lay my hand on my lord, because he is the Lord's anointed.'

See, my father, look at this piece of your robe in my hand!"

Let's stop right there and look a little bit deeper. There is more to the story than we are seeing. Backtrack to the book of Numbers, chapter 15, verse 37: "The Lord said to Moses, 'Speak to the Israelites and say to them: 'Throughout the generations to come you are to make tassels on the corners of your garments with a blue cord on each tassel.'" The significance of this tassel, or tzitziyot, is that it is to serve as a reminder of the 613 commandments given to the Israelites, primarily listed in the Torah. In Old Testament times, every Jewish person would have these tassels on their clothing, though in modern times, it is primarily limited to temple garb.

Being a reminder of God's expectations on their lives, as a part of the Jewish funeral service, the tzitziyot would be cut off of the deceased person's clothing as a symbol that they are no longer expected to uphold God's requirements. This removing of the corner of their clothing is a mark of the dead, and when David cut the corner off of Saul's clothing, it was a statement that Saul's life was truly in his hands, yet he chose mercy. Regardless of his act of grace, David still did feel remorse due to the severity of the implication of cutting off Saul's tzitziyot.

So, did Saul acknowledge David's "nice shot?" In verse 16, we see that Saul wept, and in verse 17, he admits that David is more righteous than he is. Sounds like David's act of peace hit home, and that same conviction should be on all of us when someone shows us the same courtesy.

Use the space below to add your thoughts, experiences, and convictions to make this message more personal for your audience.

Day 27: Take Heed

Key Verse(s): Jeremiah 1:14
"The Lord said to me, 'From the north disaster will be poured out on all who live in the land."

Raise your hand if I gave you a warning in class today. I don't mean a warning as if you were in trouble, but rather, a warning about something you may have been doing wrong. Raise your hand if I said any of the following to you today:

- You are over rotating your kick and getting too close to the person next to you.
- Bring your hands back up while sparring.
- Watch out for the other students as you are running.
- Look before you turn on your kata, or you will bump into the person next to you.
- Watch your control on your sparring.

As you can see, warnings are most often intended for both your safety and the safety of others around you. Because of this, it would be wise to listen to and heed those warnings.

The Bible is FULL of warnings from God, prophets, wise counselors, and so many more people, and unfortunately, most of those warnings went unheeded. Let's start at the point where Israel was split into two nations. Solomon, David's son, had just passed away, and his son Rehoboam was off to a rough start. His people pleaded for him to lighten their work load, and despite the wise council he received from the elders to respect their ask, he instead decided to make them work even harder. The ending result was that he lost ten of his twelve tribes, and the northernmost part of his country became "Israel", led by Jeroboam, while his existing kingdom remained "Judah."

Along those lines, Jeroboam was warned by a prophet named Ahijah to stay faithful to God, and yet it wasn't long before he had set up idols in Israel, completely disregarding God's laws and setting a pattern of evil kings that followed him.

Both countries were guilty, though Judah had a few kings that were righteous. One of which was Josiah, who had brought major religious reform to his country, removing idols and inspiring a revival of their nation while he reigned.

Eventually though, both countries suffered judgement. Israel was conquered by the Assyrian empire after repeated warnings to return to God, and we find ourselves in today's verse where a prophet named Jeremiah was warned that the judgement Israel experienced was about to spill over onto Judah as well. In fact, Jeremiah tried to warn the current king of Judah, Zedekiah, that he should surrender to the Babylonian empire, but again, we see an unheeded warning as he tried to flee instead. Because of this, Judah was completely given over to the Babylonians, who destroyed the city and took away the survivors as slaves, where they remained for the next 70 years.

The moral of the story is as easy as it looks: Heed warnings, especially when they come from someone wiser than yourself or someone who genuinely cares for your safety and well-being. Your challenge this week is to find an area at home that you usually struggle with in the way of obedience, and resolve to accept the wisdom from your parents without arguing or complaining.

Use the space below to add your thoughts, experiences, and convictions to make this message more personal for your audience.

Day 28: What's That Name?

Key Verse(s): Genesis 2:20
"So the man gave names to all the livestock, the birds in the sky and all the wild animals."

If I were speaking in Japanese, I would refer to myself as sensei and to all of you as karate-ka. If I were speaking in Korean, I would call myself sabim and all of you haksaeng. If I were in the Philippines, I would be called guro, and you would all be estudyante.

Our personal names are so much more than just that, however. They not only label us, but they identify us as well. Your name says that you are loved by your parents. It says which family you belong to. It says that someone cares enough about you to add meaning to your life.

In our key verse today, we see the power behind identifying others as demonstrated by Adam who was tasked to name all of the creatures on the earth. Our names belong to us; they become a representation of everything we are, inside and out. It's one of the things that cannot be taken from us – or can it?

Remember last week when we talked about Babylon conquering Judah? If we go to Daniel chapter 1, we see that the besieging of Judah began under the reign of Jehoiakim (who was taken off to Babylon with the first round of prisoners). For history buffs, this was before Zedekiah took the throne.

For the cream of the crop captives, that is, those who were physically without defects, intelligent, healthy, and good-looking, King Nebuchadnezzar wanted to keep them on hand to work in his palace. But first, they had to be stripped of their identities and given new ones so as to "remake" them his own. This included physical alteration, re-education, control over their diet, and most importantly, renaming them. Their very identities as God's people were being taken away as they were given new names to reflect the life the king wanted for them and his desire to have them forget their previous life, their God, and their family traditions. In essence, he was forcing them to conform to Babylon's way of life.

For example, the name given to Daniel was Belteshazzar, which means "Bel protects his life." His friends were given the following:

Hananiah – Shadrach (command of Aku, the Babylonian god of the moon)
Mishael – Meshach (literally translates to "who is what Aku is?")
Azariah – Abednego (servant of Nebo)

As you read all throughout the book of Daniel, you will see that these men may have had their circumstances (and names) changed, but never did they waver on their faith or loyalty of the one true God. Their dedication to continuing to eat Biblically clean foods (kosher) as listed in their dietary laws (kashrut) in the book of Leviticus was just the beginning. They also refused to bow down to the idols of Babylon, as well as to the kings themselves when it was required. Most inspiring of all was that they continued to pray to and put their faith in God, even when their very lives were threatened. So, my question to all of you is, "What's in a name?"

Use the space below to add your thoughts, experiences, and convictions to make this message more personal for your audience.

Day 29: Writing on the Wall

Key Verse(s): Daniel 5:22-23
"'But you, Belshazzar, his son, have not humbled yourself, though you knew all this. Instead, you have set yourself up against the Lord of heaven. You had the goblets from his temple brought to you, and you and your nobles, your wives and your concubines drank wine from them. You praised the gods of silver and gold, of bronze, iron, wood and stone, which cannot see or hear or understand. But you did not honor the God who holds in his hand your life and all your ways."

Who has heard the old adage, "Pride comes before a fall?" What does it mean? *(Allow students to answer)* I am in a unique position as a martial arts instructor because this art tends to bring in the best of the best, as well as the worst of the worst when it comes to pride. I've seen many people demonstrate humility over the years, but others I've seen succumb to the temptation of pride. Unfortunately, I see it in my classes from time to time as well. It's usually easy to spot, but sometimes it comes under the guise of attention-seeking, incessant hunger for praise, being overly rough with other students, pushing your way up the rank line, and the desire to always "come out on top" in sparring. All of those things can point to a problem with pride.

In today's verse, we read about Nebuchadnezzar's grandson, Belshazzar, who had a massive problem with pride himself. We find him in the throws of a massive banquet he is hosting, when he commands that the sacred goblets from the temple of God be brought in simply so that they can drink more wine with them and praise the idols of gold, silver, bronze, iron, wood, and stone. (Apparently, he didn't take the first commandment seriously).

In the middle of the party, however, human fingers appeared and began writing something on the wall. Belshazzar was understandably afraid and tried to get his wise men to translate the words on his wall, but they could not. His wife referred Daniel, who was known for translating dreams and signs, and he was summoned promptly.

With God's help, Daniel was able to decipher the writing and the meaning in verse 26: "'Here is what these words mean: Mene: God has numbered the days of your reign and brought it to an end. Tekel: You have been weighed on the scales and found wanting. Peres: Your Kingdom is divided and given to the Medes and Persians.'"

Unfortunately, Belshazzar did not have much time to ponder or prepare for this warning of impending doom, for that same evening, he was killed, and Darius the Mede took over his kingdom.

Students, it's time to check your heart with a fine-toothed comb. Is there any pride lurking in there that you can rid yourself of? If in doubt, meditate on Psalm 139:23-24 this week: "Search me, God, and know my heart; test me and know my anxious thoughts. See if there is any offensive way in me, and lead me in the way everlasting."

Use the space below to add your thoughts, experiences, and convictions to make this message more personal for your audience.

_____

_____

_____

_____

_____

_____

_____

_____

_____

_____

_____

_____

_____

_____

_____

Day 30: The Heavens Declare

Key Verse(s): Psalm 19:1-2
"The heavens declare the glory of God; the skies proclaim the work of his hands. Day after day they pour forth speech; night after night they reveal knowledge."

Raise your hands if you like to stargaze at night. What was the most interesting thing you've ever seen in the night sky? As for myself, I've seen shooting stars, blood moons, a solar eclipse, and more. You might be wondering what this has to do with the martial arts, right? I may not have hard evidence to back it up, but I have my speculations about heavenly events, and one of them tends to impact our classes in an interesting way.

I know that when the moon is full, I typically see an elevated level of energy in class, as well as a lack of self-control. In fact, I've resolved myself to try to avoid sparring on full moon nights, unless I have a high level of trust in the students in the class. Could this be because the moon is said to influence the tides? After all, we are made up of roughly 55-75% water, depending on age and gender.

The Bible has many stories about signs in the sky, but there is a fine line between relying on the stars for your daily news (which is Biblically considered a sin), and looking to the stars to see the glory of the Lord portrayed in His creation.

Today, let's take a look at one of the most famous stories in the Bible about stars, but first, we'll take a quick stop in possibly the oldest book of the Bible. Job 9:9 says, "He is the Maker of the Bear and Orion, the Pleiades and the constellations of the south." If God made the stars and everything else in the sky, surely, this is another way He can glorify himself when science confirms the word of the Bible.

So, what story do you think I am referring to? I'll give you a hint: wise men were following a star. Of course, I am referring to the story of Jesus' birth!

What's amazing about this story is that modern day studies have gathered more information surrounding the star of Bethlehem, and the results are awe-inspiring. Using the original studies of Johannes Kepler, many astronomy tracking devices have been made that can accurately model the position of the stars at the time of Jesus' birth. Furthermore, a lawyer by the name of Frederick Larson embarked on a journey to share his findings on the subject, and his results bring it all back to the true word of God.

For starters, during the time that Mary was being told by Gabriel that she would conceive and bear a son (see Luke 1:31), the stars were already foretelling of something great to come. You see, Jupiter (the king planet) was circling around Regulus (king star) in the virgin constellation. Jupiter's circling motion was more of the shape of a halo than a circle, however, which indicates an action of "the king planet" crowning "the king star." More interestingly, just under the virgin constellation's foot was a new moon, symbolizing new life. As Revelations 12:1 says: "A great sign appeared in heaven: a woman clothed with the sun, with the moon under her feet and a crown of twelve stars on her head."

Fast forward about 9 months, and the "star" that the wise men were seeking was not just one star, but a conjunction of Jupiter (the king planet), and Venus (the mother planet) right over Bethlehem and in the lion constellation (see Hosea 5:14: "For I will be like a lion to Ephraim, like a great lion to Judah...").

Jesus' birth was foretold in the sky exactly how God said it would be in His word, thousands of years before it happened. And this is just one of many stories about signs and wonders performed in the heavens by God. I encourage you all this week to comb Scripture yourself and see if you can find another story of God's creation bringing the glory back to Him.

Use the space below to add your thoughts, experiences, and convictions to make this message more personal for your audience.

Day 31: Class Rules

Key Verse(s): Nehemiah 9:38
"'In view of all this, we are making a binding agreement, putting it in writing, and our leaders, our Levites and our priests are affixing their seals to it.'"

*****Instructors, please have printed copies of your dojo rules for students to take home after today's devotion*****

When was the last time you all have read over our class rules and etiquette sheet? For some of you, maybe you read it when you first signed up and didn't give it another glance since then. I would like to hope that some of you take a look at it from time to time to refresh yourself on my expectations for your behavior and etiquette in class. On it, you will find many rules that help maintain a safe, courteous environment, like:

- Students will bow, as a form of respect, upon entering and leaving the dojo floor.
-Students should never pass between a black belt and other students.
- After being directly instructed, the student should bow to the teacher with a "yes ma'am" or "thank you sir."
- Students should be very respectful and quiet while they observe others sparring or testing.
- Always wait for commands before attempting to practice techniques – this is important for the safety of the students standing around you.

Those are just a few of the class rules we have! Speaking of which, I would like all of you to take a copy of our class rules with you tonight and read over them with your parents before class next week. It's always important to remember the class expectations so that you don't forget what you are responsible for.

That brings us to today's key verse, in which we find God's chosen people home again in Jerusalem after 70 years of captivity in Babylon. The temple was reconstructed, the city walls were rebuilt, and it was time to get their spiritual affairs in order once again.

Ezra led the people in a revival of their faith, first reading God's law to the people over the course of two weeks. After hearing God's expectations for their lives, the Israelites made a promise to God that they would obey His laws moving forward. Their sentiment to honor God was a new covenant that cleansed their nation and set the stage for the same Jerusalem where the Messiah would hold the Last Supper just over 500 years later.

This week, I challenge all of you to review our class rules and commit as many of them to memory as you can. I would love to see what that looks like in action next week!

Use the space below to add your thoughts, experiences, and convictions to make this message more personal for your audience.

Day 32: Achilles' Heel

Key Verse(s): Judges 16:16-17
"With such nagging she prodded him day after day until he was sick to death of it. So he told her everything. 'No razor has ever been used on my head,' he said, 'because I have been a Nazirite dedicated to God from my mother's womb. If my head were shaved, my strength would leave me, and I would become as weak as any other man.'"

I have a question for you all: What is your weak spot while sparring? Everyone has something they can improve on, and until you have mastered that weakness, it leaves an area where you are vulnerable. Do you tend to drop your hands, leaving your head exposed? Do you lean in with your head too often? Do you keep your feet planted and not make use of your footwork? How about this one: Do any of you turn your heads away from your sparring partner? Or do you let your emotions get the best of you when you know you should be keeping your cool?

The truth is, no one is going to be perfect at sparring, but you have to realize your weaknesses so that you can improve them and compensate for them.

We see numerous occasions in the Bible where someone had a particular weakness. For example, in Genesis 32:24, we read that Jacob (soon to be Israel) was wrestling with God through the night. In verse 25, it says, "When the man saw that he could not overpower him (Jacob), he touched the socket of Jacob's hip so that his hip was wrenched as he wrestled with the man." This is the reason, incidentally, why the sciatic nerve area is not permitted for consumption in Jewish dietary laws. Hence, hind quarters are excluded in kosher cooking practices.

In today's verses, we read a story about Samson who, strong as he was, had a significant weakness. Does anyone know this story? What was his weak spot? (Allow students to answer) It was girls. It would seem Samson was a man who wore his heart on his sleeve, and he didn't always keep his guard up when it came to the ladies.

Delilah knew this full well and took advantage of Samson's

vulnerability. Secretly, she was helping the Philistines capture Samson, so once he admitted to her that cutting his hair would make him as weak as any other man, she ran to the Philistine rulers and divulged the juicy information.

While Samson was sleeping on her lap, Delilah called someone to cut off his hair, and when he awoke, sure enough, his strength had left him (verse 19).

Samson was arrested, blinded, bound, and sent to Gaza as a prisoner all because he had put his faith in the wrong person. Later on, God did allow his strength to return to him one last time, and it was then that he braced himself between the Philistine temple pillars and brought them down, collapsing the temple and killing everyone inside.

I have one last question for everyone: When you have one side that is weaker than the other, what do I ask you to do? You work that side twice as hard so that it is as strong as it can be. This week, my challenge to all of you is to pray about where your weaknesses lie and try to strengthen them so that your Achilles' heel isn't quite so vulnerable.

Use the space below to add your thoughts, experiences, and convictions to make this message more personal for your audience.

Day 33: Still, Small Voice

Key Verse(s): 1 Kings 19:11-13
"The Lord said, 'Go out and stand on the mountain in the presence of the Lord, for the Lord is about to pass by.' Then a great and powerful wind tore the mountains apart and shattered the rocks before the Lord, but the Lord was not in the wind. After the wind there was an earthquake, but the Lord was not in the earthquake. After the earthquake came a fire, but the Lord was not in the fire. And after the fire came a gentle whisper. When Elijah heard it, he pulled his cloak over his face and went out and stood at the mouth of the cave. Then a voice said to him, 'What are you doing here, Elijah?'"

One of the things I really love about our mat time is that it allows me the opportunity to speak to attentive ears. Students, would you say you give me that same level of attentiveness during class as well? Or are we saving the "best for last," so to speak?

I will say, there is a lot more chattering going on during class than there should be, and I (and the other instructors) would be ecstatic if we had this level of focus while working out. Quieting yourself to pay attention is not just for your safety, but it is a sign of respect to all of us, who are trying to give you the benefit of our knowledge for the short time we get to see you each week. It doesn't make sense that this time should be wasted with us reminding you to stay quiet so that you can hear our instructions, when it could be better utilized practicing and evaluating. After all, there's plenty of time before and after class for all the chatter!

In today's verses, we find a desperate Elijah on the run. King Ahab (one of the evil kings of Israel), and his wife Jezebel had been killing God's prophets simply for doing what God called them to do. Understandably, Elijah was desperate to escape their wrath.

While trying to stay ahead of his pursuers, Elijah had his needs provided for by an angel sent by God. Remember that "Yahweh Jireh" means "the Lord will provide."

In the midst of uncertainty, however, God calls Elijah to

stand on the mountain in His presence. Our key verses say that God sent a powerful wind, an earthquake, and a fire, but the Lord was not in any of these. It was in a gentle whisper that God spoke to Elijah in.

I think that is such a beautiful picture. God was demonstrating His power and authority over the earth, and yet, to hear Him, Elijah had to first quiet himself and listen. How many of you do that? How many of you take the time to quiet yourselves, slow down, and really listen to what God has for you?

One of the benefits to living in modern times is all of the wonderful distractions available to us. There are video games, televisions, amusement parks, parties, playdates, sports, and everything else in between, but in truth, while some of those things may be beneficial, it is in the quiet that we hear God the loudest. Along these lines, it's no surprise that we read of Jesus going off by himself to pray many times in the New Testament. It is because He knew that to hear God, sometimes you have to eliminate the distractions and just listen.

My challenge to all of you this week is to take some time out of your busy schedules to find a quiet room to go to and just listen to what God has for you. You won't regret making that time for His word to find you.

Use the space below to add your thoughts, experiences, and convictions to make this message more personal for your audience.

Day 34: It's in the Details

Key Verse(s): Mark 15:37
"With a loud cry, Jesus breathed his last."

When I watch your katas, does it seem as if I always have a list of things for you to work on? Once in a while, you may make a big mistake such as turning the wrong way or completely forgetting the kata. More often than not, however, it is the details I am correcting. I pick at the ready hands, the stances, the placement of your blocks and strikes, when you yell, and whether or not you step backwards on goman. You see, most people can learn a kata correctly, but it's in the details that you truly see how adept someone is at what they are doing.

In today's verse, we come to a very hard day. Jesus' death on the cross for all of our sins is one of the hardest things to grasp because in one sense, you know it was necessary, but in another, you wish it either didn't happen – or even better, you wish it didn't *have to* happen. It was the sins of the world that held Him to that cross, and His love for us despite that hits my heart in a way that nothing else can.

We all know the most important aspect of the story, but do you ever look at the other details? Sometimes, it's those details that speak almost as loudly as the event itself, and here are just a few:

- The 300+ prophecies that were fulfilled about Jesus' death and resurrection were made close to 1,000 years before Jesus' crucifixion. For example, David wrote in Psalm 22:18, "They divide my clothes among them and cast lots for my garment." This prophecy was fulfilled in Luke 23:34.
- The day Jesus was crucified: Historians have used various clues in the Bible, such as the specific timing of Passover, the reign of Pontius Pilate, and the fact that Jesus had to be taken off the cross before Shabbat (Sabbath) began. They have dated his death as April 3rd, 33 AD, at 3:00 PM. Is there anything interesting about this date? Could it be related to the Holy Trinity? In addition, Jesus spent 6 hours on the cross. For those versed in eschatology, or the study of end times, that number

carries a special significance. Even if we omit those numerical details, the fact that Jesus died on Passover, a Jewish festival in remembrance that the blood of the lamb was poured out to save the Israelites from death, carries significant meaning!

- As Jesus died, the temple veil tore in two pieces from the *top* to the *bottom*. This is very significant, for the veil was considered the one thing that separated mankind from the presence of God. In addition, the veil was approximately four inches thick and made with many layers of thread. This was not something any man could have done. Furthermore, the symbolism of it tearing from the top to the bottom signifies God instigating the access mankind would now have to heaven; it is not something that man could muscle through on his own. Ephesians 2:8-9 states, "For it is by grace you have been saved, through faith – and this is not from yourselves, it is the gift of God – not by works, so that no one can boast."

- There was a lunar eclipse, aka a blood moon. Though blood moons were common during Jewish festivals because of the timing of the festivals, we can't dispute that God has used stellar events as signs all throughout history.

- Mark 27:51-53 also recounts an earthquake just after Jesus gave up his spirit. "The earth shook, the rocks split and the tombs broke open. The bodies of many holy people who had died were raised to life. They came out of the tombs after Jesus' resurrection and went into the holy city and appeared to many people."

As you can see, there was so much more to this story than meets the eye. As with all things God ordains, you will see His fingerprint in every intentional facet of the bigger picture. This week, I encourage you all to read through the Easter story with your parents to see if you can find more details glorifying God and this holy day.

Use the space below to add your thoughts, experiences, and convictions to make this message more personal for your audience.

Day 35: True Balance

Key Verse(s): James 2:17
"In the same way, faith by itself, if it is not accompanied by action, is dead."

Jhoon Rhee, the "Father of American Tae Kwon Do", shared this amazing art with America in 1956. His ideas of the balance of mind, body, and spirit have been the foundation of so many instructors' teachings. You may recognize one of Mr. Rhee's most famous quotes: "A balanced education consists of knowledge in the mind, honesty in the heart, and strength in the body." Does this sound familiar? For my students, it should! We say this at the end of every class, and for good reason. As I have said many times, a true martial artist fosters a true balance of all three facets of training, not just one or two.

The idea of balance is very much rooted in cultures all over the world, and today, we will talk about one that is emphasized in the Jewish culture called Sukkot, or Feast of Tabernacles. Beginning on the 15th of the Jewish month Tishrei (September-October timeframe for Christians), this God-appointed festival is to commemorate the Israelite's time in the desert as they were waiting to enter the promised land. During this time, the Israelites lived in temporary tents and moved about often, but they were guided and protected by God the entire time.

Because this festival also fell around the time of late harvesting, it had also taken on aspects of thanksgiving in the Lord's providence, much like the Christian celebration of Thanksgiving in November. Four typical harvests for this time of year are represented in the nightly blessings, including palm branches (lulav), citron (etrog), myrtle (hadas), and willow (arava), which are bound together and waved in all four directions to symbolize their gratitude for God's provision, as well as His omnipresence all over the world.

As I've mentioned before, the biggest truth is in the details, for each of these plants have a symbolic meaning. The willow, which has neither smell nor taste, symbolizes one who lacks knowledge and good deeds. The myrtle, which smells good but does not have a taste, symbolizes someone that has good deeds but no knowledge. The palm branch has a pleasant taste but no smell, which symbolizes someone with knowledge but no good deeds. Lastly, the citron has both a nice fragrance and taste, which is symbolic of one who has knowledge and good deeds to back it up. The important takeaway of this symbolism is that one should have both the knowledge of God's laws *and* good deeds to back it up.

If we look at today's verse, we see the New Testament version of this very same lesson. "Faith by itself, if it is not accompanied by action, is dead." If we skip to verse 18, James expounds with: "Show me your faith without deeds, and I will show you my faith by my deeds." Touche'!

So let's bring in today's mat time. How useful is knowledge if you don't put it into action? Or if you lack the goodness in your heart to use that information for good? Is strength good to have if you have no knowledge of how to use it? Or what if you are strong, but your heart is not in the right place? What if you have a good heart, but you never study or work out your body? As you can see, you need all three to achieve balance in all things.

This week, I challenge you all to contemplate if you are lacking in any of the three areas. If you feel convicted to make a change, it's better to get on that right away.

Use the space below to add your thoughts, experiences, and convictions to make this message more personal for your audience.

Day 36: Eyes on Jesus

Key Verse(s): Matthew 14:30
"But when he saw the wind, he was afraid and, beginning to sink, cried out, 'Lord, save me!'"

Raise your hands if you get nervous on your test day. What is it that you are worried about? Perhaps you think you won't pass, or maybe you won't do as well as you know you can. Are you hesitant to get up in front of a crowd and have all eyes on you as you try to remember your katas, blocks, one-steps, and more in front of everyone? As strange as this sounds, even I still get nervous when I test! But my reasons may be different from all of yours. *(Fill in any reasons you may be nervous or hesitant to test when you are recommended for doing so.)*

Today's mat time topic is just as much for all of you as it is for myself. In Matthew 14, we read a story about a miraculous event. Do you all remember the story of Jesus feeding thousands with only two fish and five loaves of bread? Immediately after this event, Jesus went up the mountain to pray by himself overnight while the disciples got into their boat on the shore. Verse 34 points out that there was a strong wind that was tossing the boat about, so likely, the disciples were already feeling a bit anxious. But in verse 25, we read, "Shortly before dawn Jesus went out to them, walking on the lake." Imagine how they felt, seeing a man walking on the surface of the waves calmly, when they were getting tossed about. But when Jesus identified himself and told them not to be afraid, Peter stated in verse 28, "Lord, if it's you, tell me to come to you on the water." This was a bold statement of trust. Being a fisherman, Peter likely spent most of his life on the water and knew better than most the impossibility of walking across the surface of the sea. To believe that Jesus could do it is one thing, but to have faith that you can also do it through Him is an entirely different matter. Still, he placed his fate in Jesus' hands to do the impossible as He told him, "Come." (Philippians 4:13 would have looked great here!)

Keeping his eyes fixed on Jesus alone, Peter left his comfort zone and was able to walk on the water, but it was when he took his eyes off of his Savior (and focused on the winds) that he began to sink.

If we stop right here, there is a very important truth nugget that we should always remember: With your eyes on Jesus, you can do the impossible, but if you take your eyes off of Him, the world, your fears, and uncertainty will distract you from all things you are capable of through Christ. Raise your hands if you have ever been in that place?

The good news is that we don't have to worry. God knows our hearts, and He gives us comfort in His word. Verse 31 reads: "Immediately Jesus reached out his hand and caught him." Even when we falter, Jesus will never leave our sides.

With all of the challenges in our lives, including those of the past and present, and in the "winds" to come, we simply have to remember that if we want to walk on water, we will ultimately have to take a leap of faith to first get out of the boat.

Use the space below to add your thoughts, experiences, and convictions to make this message more personal for your audience.

Day 37: Behemoth

Key Verse(s): Job 40:15
"Look at Behemoth, which I made along with you and which feeds on grass like an ox."

Chinese culture is rich with dragon-lore and symbols that are displayed in all manner of their lives from building décor, dances, feng shui practices, statues, costumes, artwork, carvings, and more. To the Chinese, a dragon is a symbol of great power, wisdom, wealth, and good fortune. Chinese dragons, simply called "lo'ng" are considered to primarily live in lakes and rivers, and they represent the "east" cardinal direction, where the sun rises. They are even considered to be greater than the emperor himself, and as such, you will see many depictions of dragons in palaces and in the famous Forbidden City.

Dragon lore isn't just limited to China, however! Countries all over the world have their own legends and depictions of this elusive creature, and the names are just as various:

Danish – Drage
Italian – Drago
Korean – Yong
Russian – Drakon
Hebrew – Tanniyn

The Hebrew word above roughly translates to "land or sea monsters or serpents", and aptly so, for each country has their own historical accounts that vary from land to sea. Historical figures like Marco Polo, John of Damascus, Athanasius Kircher, Alexander the Great, Job and so many more all have references to these creatures recorded in history, but the question still begs, "Are dragons real? (Or were they?)"

As with all things, we need look no further than in the Bible, for there are numerous mentions of "leviathan", "behemoth", "serpent dragon", "fiery flying serpent", and so many more in the books of Daniel, Jeremiah, Ezekiel, Micah, Malachi, Job, and Isaiah.

If these great beasts existed, where are they now? Perhaps

the better question is *what were they*? Many Biblical scientists agree that the exaggerated accounts of these beasts all reference the same creatures: Dinosaurs. Let's look at Job's entire account in chapter 40: "Look at Behemoth, which I made along with you and which feeds on grass like an ox. What strength it has in its loins, what power in the muscles of its belly! Its tail sways like a cedar; the sinews of its thighs are close-knit. Its bones are tubes of bronze, its limbs like rods of iron. It ranks first among the works of God, yet its Maker can approach it with his sword. The hills bring it their produce, and all the wild animals play nearby. Under the lotus plants it lies, hidden among the reeds in the marsh. The lotuses conceal it in their shadow; the poplars by the stream surround it. A raging river does not alarm it; it is secure, though the Jordan should surge against its mouth."

What do you think students? Is it possible that dragons were dinosaurs? My challenge to all of you this week is to look over Scripture with your families and see if you can find similar accounts that back the word of God. I think if you look deep enough, you will find that is just the case.

Use the space below to add your thoughts, experiences, and convictions to make this message more personal for your audience.

Day 38: A Harvest

Key Verse(s): Matthew 13:23
"But the seed falling on good soil refers to someone who hears the word and understands it. This is the one who produces a crop, yielding a hundred, sixty or thirty times what was sown."

Students, each week we carve out the last bit of class to do our mat time, but why, do you think it is so important we have this time? Is it because I just want to use up the last few minutes of class? Is it so we can have a few minutes of quiet contemplation? What do you think? *(Allow students to answer)*

The truth is, our mat time is a very special time where I get to combine what I love – God, and the martial arts – and plant seeds of truth that I hope one day will bring in a harvest. You might be thinking, "where's the dirt?" But for my older students and parents, you may already know exactly what I'm talking about.

Jesus, too, spoke in parables many times during his earthly ministry, and today, we're going to talk about one of the most famous ones, which can be found in Matthew 13. In this parable, Jesus talks about four types of seeds that were scattered in a farmer's field:

- Some of the seeds fell along the path, and the birds ate it up right away. This is symbolic of God's word falling on someone, and the enemy immediately snatching away what they learned.
- Some fell on rocky places where it began to grow, but then withered because there was no place to take root. This refers to someone who hears the Gospel, receives it, but does not "take root" in their faith. When trouble comes, they quickly backtrack and fall out of the faith.
- Still, more seed fell in the midst of thorns, which grew but was eventually choked out by their prickly neighbors. This group refers to someone who hears and grows in the Word, but the "worries of this life and the deceitfulness of wealth choke the word, making it unfruitful." (Verse 22)
- The last type of seed fell on good soil, where it produced many more times what was originally sown. This is symbolic of the

one who receives the word, grows in their faith, and bears fruit that will, in turn, plant more seeds and yield more harvest in the future.

It seems simple enough, but the truth is our hearts can be incredibly deceptive. While we think we may be fruitful, or faithful to God, we may just be getting choked out by the world around us.

I like to imagine this lesson as a big picture of a tree. Our emotions, thoughts, and beliefs make up the inconspicuous roots, and whether or not those are in the right place, we may or may not have a healthy tree trunk with branches above ground (what everyone else can see). Our behaviors are the trunk of the tree, which decides the health of the branches – are they bare, brittle and dry? Or are they full of lush, green leaves and fruit? Which scenario do you think is God's will for our lives? Which is Satan's?

My challenge to all of you is to draw a picture of this special tree and bring it to class for me to see next week. In addition, I would like all of you to pray about the type of plant in our story you strive to be most like.

Use the space below to add your thoughts, experiences, and convictions to make this message more personal for your audience.

Day 39: A Job Well Done

Key Verse(s) Revelation 22:3
"No longer will there be any curse. The throne of God and of
the Lamb will be in the city, and his servants will serve him."

Students, we unfortunately live in a world where knowledge
of the martial arts is crucial so that each of us knows how to
defend not only ourselves, but our family and friends in time of
need. As much as I would like to believe otherwise, there are a
lot of bad people sharing this space we call earth, and not all of
them are safe to be around. It's an unfortunate reality of living
in a fallen world, but it hasn't always been so, nor will it always
be this way.

When God created the world, it was first without any sin.
Because of this, there were so many differences between then
and now that it's almost impossible to imagine what life must
have been like. In fact, I have an idea, and it's really what the
Bible tells me about the new Heaven we will all be living in one
day.

Let's look at some of these differences:

- Many Biblical scholars agree that there was no rain on the
earth until after the Great Flood. If we look at Genesis 2:5-6, it
states, "the Lord God had not sent rain on the earth" and
"streams came up from the earth and watered the whole surface
of the ground." After Noah's flood, however, there was regular
rain.

- The Bible also alludes to animals and mankind being
vegetarian, or not eating meat. Genesis 1:29 says, "Then God
said, 'I give you every seed-bearing plant on the face of the
whole earth and every tree that has fruit with seed in it. They
will be yours for food'". Verse 30 also goes on to say that for
animals, God gave "every green plant for food" as well.
Imagine that! That means there were no predators, and no
worry of wild animals either. Fast forward to post-flood times,
and Genesis 9:3 says, "Everything that lives and moves about
will be food for you", likely due to the shortage of plant life.
(The book of Leviticus also specifies which meats are clean for

God's chosen people as well).
- Pre-flood, mankind lived much, much longer than we do today. For example, in Genesis 5, we see three people that lived a very long time, yet in modern times, living to be 100 years old seems to be quite the accomplishment. Let's compare that to some of our Old Testament men:

- Mahalalel – 895 years (verse 17)
- Jared – 962 years (verse 20)
- Methuselah – 969 years (verse 27)

One of the biggest changes, however, came with the sin of eating the forbidden fruit in the Garden of Eden. In addition to being banned from the garden, God states in Genesis 3:17, "Cursed is the ground because of you; through painful toil you will eat food from it all the days of your life." This brought the concept of hard, manual labor, physical (and spiritual) thorns on plants (and in life), and personal responsibility for oneself.

The good news is if we look at today's key verse, we see there will no longer be any of these curses in Heaven. Biblical scholars believe we will still perform work, but it will be through joyful acts of service, rather than the manual labor we are subject to now. If God takes our talents into account, I think I'll be out of a job in Heaven! There won't be a need for martial arts instructors anymore, because no one will need to defend themselves. As crazy as it sounds, I can't wait until that day!

Use the space below to add your thoughts, experiences, and convictions to make this message more personal for your audience.

_____

_____

_____

_____

_____

_____

_____

_____

_____

_____

_____

_____

_____

_____

_____

_____

_____

Day 40: Strong in the Lord

Key Verse(s): Ephesians 6:10-13
"Finally, be strong in the Lord and in his mighty power. Put on the full armor of God, so that you can take your stand against the devil's schemes. For our struggle is not against flesh and blood, but against the rulers, against the authorities, against the powers of this dark world and against the spiritual forces of evil in the heavenly realms. Therefore put on the full armor of God, so that when the day of evil comes, you may be able to stand your ground, and after you have done everything, to stand."

For most people interested in the martial arts, I have found that their primary interests in training has to do with (1) their desire to be stronger and (2) their hope of becoming more skilled in defending themselves. There are so many other reasons, but those are definitely the ones I see most often. Along these lines, history books are full of people who have devoted their lives to training in the martial arts for the same desire to be able to stand against a foe that they may encounter one day. The idea of having a physical vulnerability is very sobering to some, and the martial arts (or any fighting art) provides a sense of security over people who are not trained.

Today's verse, however, reminds us that the true battle before us is not one of "flesh and blood, but against the rulers, against the authorities, against the powers of this dark world and against the spiritual forces of evil in the heavenly realms."

Have you ever been picked on at school? Have you ever gotten in a fight with a sibling? Have you ever felt like you had to defend yourself against someone else? Guess what? That person may have been close to you physically, but have you considered that the enemy of God is behind it all? Have you ever thought to fight against the one who inspires so many people to do and say harmful things on this earth? Do you all know who I'm talking about?

If "our struggle is not against flesh and blood", then we need to take a deeper look to learn how to properly engage in spiritual warfare with this enemy. But how do we fight such a battle?

Over the next several weeks, we are going to be taking a closer look at some very specific tools that God has given us to help fight this enemy and stand firm in our faith during the process. What are these amazing tools? Can anyone tell me about some of them? *(Allow students to answer)*

We are talking about the armor of God. I will give you a brief overview of them today, and we will be going more in depth about them over the next few weeks:

- The Belt of Truth
-The Breastplate of Righteousness
- The Gospel Shoes of Peace
-The Shield of Faith
- The Helmet of Salvation
- The Sword of the Spirit

The good news is that God's word tells us exactly how to implement and utilize each of these pieces of equipment, but it is our duty to make sure that we are fully armed. If just one piece of this armor is missing, you allow the enemy a way to take advantage of your weakness. After all, this isn't about a battle between two men; it is a battle between two worlds.

Use the space below to add your thoughts, experiences, and convictions to make this message more personal for your audience.

Day 41: The Belt of Truth

Key Verse(s): Ephesians 6:14
"Stand firm, then, with the belt of truth buckled around your waist…"

Students, what do you wear over your uniforms each week in class? *(Allow students to answer – belt)* That's right, it is your belt! What is interesting about your belt is that it holds your uniform in place while you work out. In the same way, a belt was one of the first things a soldier would put on before any other equipment because it was crucial for holding together the rest of their armor. For example, the breastplate would hook into it, and without a breastplate, your chest and heart would be exposed. It also had a place to hold your sword, which would be crucial for active engagement with the enemy.

Truth is another way of saying reality, which means if we are going to put on a belt of truth, it is important for us to always speak truth to those around us, as well as to ourselves. But in a very busy world, full of distractions, where can we find truth that doesn't try to sway our hearts? Who can we go to for truth that doesn't have an agenda or dishonest intentions behind their answer? God's word!

To understand God's word, we have to get into it and commit it to memory. The world is always waiting right around the corner to try to trick us and make us doubt the validity of the Bible, and it's up to us to have that discernment and understanding. Remember Jesus' words in Matthew 7:13-14: "Enter through the narrow gate. For wide is the gate and broad is the road that leads to destruction, and many enter through it. But small is the gate and narrow the road that leads to life, and only a few find it." This tells us that there are many falsehoods in this world that may sound nice, but only one truth. Jesus warns us about some of them in verse 15: "Watch out for false prophets. They come to you in sheep's clothing, but inwardly they are ferocious wolves."

That nagging voice that whispers, "Did God *really* say that?" has been effective since Eve first took a bite of the forbidden fruit, and though it may look different in current times, it's the same deception repackaged. That is why is it so important to first have that belt of truth. Without it, we likely wouldn't think we needed to stand our ground or fight in the first place. And even worse, we could be misleading others right alongside us.

When you put on your karate belts each week, I want it to be a reminder of today's lesson and how we each need to have truth in our hearts before engaging in any type of warfare.

Use the space below to add your thoughts, experiences, and convictions to make this message more personal for your audience.

Day 42: The Breastplate of Righteousness

Key Verse(s): Ephesians 6:14
"Stand firm then, with the belt of truth buckled around your waist, with the breastplate of righteousness in place..."

***** *Instructors, please have a sparring chest protector handy for demonstration*****

(Hold up chest protector) Students, what is this called? Different martial arts schools may or may not require a piece of sparring gear like this, but it is simply a chest protector. What would a piece of sparring gear like this protect? *(Allow students to answer)* That's right, it would protect your chest, and it also adds a layer of protection for your rib cage, liver, stomach, lungs, and most of all, your heart.

This is exactly what a soldiers' breastplate would do as well, making it a crucial part of their self-defense. If one of their vital organs was injured, they would no longer be able to fight, and the battle would be over.

The breastplate of righteousness, instead of physically protecting our chest and organs, is useful in protecting us from the inevitable sin we encounter when making poor choices. You see, righteousness means doing right in God's eyes, and doing the right thing protects us from the harm that may come back to us when we sin. Much like a boomerang, the consequences of our actions always seem to come back at us, don't they? And usually, they do so with a vengeance! But if we do the right thing, we are protecting ourselves from the biproduct of our wrongdoing.

So we laid the groundwork for righteousness, and certainly it is something we should always do our best to seek, but can we expect ourselves to *always* be perfect? I'll give you a hint: the answer is found in Romans 3:10: "As it is written: 'There is no one righteous, not even one.'" I think a lot of believers take that as a free pass to do as they please and use that verse as an excuse. "Well, I can't be perfect anyway, so of course I made a mistake!" Is that the right attitude to have? Of course not!

We must always strive to be like the One who was perfectly

righteous – Jesus. As Paul reminded us in 1 Corinthians 11:1: "Follow my example, as I follow the example of Christ." Also, 1 Peter 2:21 states: "To this you were called, because Christ suffered for you, leaving you an example, that you should follow in his steps."

Regardless of our human limitations, we should always strive to live our lives the way Jesus lived His, as much as we are able. And with those righteous acts worn as our breastplate, we can continue to engage in spiritual warfare.

Use the space below to add your thoughts, experiences, and convictions to make this message more personal for your audience.

Day 43: The Gospel Shoes of Peace

Key Verse(s): Ephesians 6:15
"...and with your feet fitted with the readiness that comes from the gospel of peace."

Students, if you have sparring gear, I want you to grab your sparring boots for our mat time today. We are going to be talking about the Gospel shoes of peace!

If you look at the bottoms of your sparring boots, what do you see? There's no bottom, of course. Do you think these would make good boots for going to war? *(Allow students to answer)* They most certainly would not!

The last couple weeks, we have been talking about different parts of a soldier's armor in Biblical times, and it's time for those shoes! There are many differences between wartime shoes and the ones you hold in your hands, but the main difference is that the soldiers often had nails sticking out of the bottom of their shoes to help them grip the ground more easily. Do any of you play soccer? What do you call those bumps on the bottom of your soccer shoes? *(Cleats)* Do cleats help keep you from slipping on the ground while you are running? This would also come in handy for a soldier who was face to face with an adversary, and the two were clashing against each other. Imagine those nails gripping the dirt and allowing the soldier to stand firm while fighting. In addition, they also helped the soldier climb up rocky hills, which was very important.

To a warrior, the right shoes were imperative, but what does peace have to do with shoes? Can anyone tell me what peace is? *(Allow students to answer)* Peace is defined as the absence of war or other hostilities, but more importantly, it is a mental state free of nervousness, fear, remorse, worry, or anxiety. Peace is knowing that regardless of what happens on this earth, you will be in Heaven with Jesus one day, and that is a truth that can only be found in the Gospel.

How can one attain this peace? If it can only be found in the good news of the Gospel, then we receive this free gift by accepting the gift of salvation that Jesus has offered us through His sacrifice on the cross. Having this peace grounds us in life much like those special shoes would ground you while in battle or when playing soccer.

But what about those who have not heard the good news of salvation? In Romans 10:14-15, Paul writes: "How, then, can they call on the one they have not believed in? And how can they believe in the one of whom they have not heard? And how can they hear without someone preaching to them? And how can anyone preach unless they are sent? As it is written: 'How beautiful are the feet of those who bring good news!'"

Students, if we have the gift of salvation, it is a gift we are called to share with others! Imagine how scary life can look to someone who has no hope. But by using the talents given to us, we can share the God of hope with others, and then they, too, can live a life of peace (and perhaps share it with someone else too)!

This week, I'd like to challenge you all to think of a way to share Jesus with one person. If you are bashful about talking to people, consider doing a kind act of service like leaving little gifts on a neighbor's porch with a Bible verse on it, or volunteering for a local ministry. Remember, actions speak louder than words!

Use the space below to add your thoughts, experiences, and convictions to make this message more personal for your audience.

Day 44: The Shield of Faith

Key Verse(s): Ephesians 6:16
"In addition to all this, take up the shield of faith, with which you can extinguish all the flaming arrows of the evil one."

*****Have a body target handy for today's mat time*****

Students, how many of you have used one of these? They are pretty thick, aren't they? Do you feel somewhat protected if you are holding one of these while your partner is kicking at you? What if you had someone kicking at you, and you didn't have one of these body targets? (That would pretty much be open sparring, wouldn't it?)

While this isn't a shield, it pretty much works like one. This target protects you from the attacks of the enemy, basically putting a buffer between you and them, and that's comforting, isn't it?

Today, we are talking about the shield of faith. Does anyone remember from our key verse what exactly the shield of faith helps us do? *(Allow students to answer)* It helps us to "extinguish all the flaming arrows of the evil one." I don't know about you, but I haven't seen any fiery arrows coming my way lately. Have any of you? So, what is this passage talking about? *(Allow input)*

Those fiery arrows can be anything that comes your way, seeking to harm you, distract you from good works, or derail you emotionally (especially during times of spiritual growth). *(Instructors, take this time to share a personal story about when you were doing something good for the kingdom and had fiery arrows raining down on you. Invite the students to do the same, but try to keep it to the point.)*

So aside from trying to stop us from doing something good that we may be doing, what other reasons would the enemy want to hurl those arrows at us? Those fiery arrows are also symbolic of temptation to sin, and Satan loves it when we slip back into sin! He purposefully tries to get us to be unkind or callous to others, he wants us to act in an unrighteous way, and he especially loves it when we disobey or use unkind words.

Then, when we're feeling bad about what we've done, he tries to plant doubts about Jesus' goodness and love for us so that in desperation, we may seek unrighteous ways of thinking. Do you see what's happening here? This is what is called a rabbit hole. At the bottom of this hole, we may even begin to believe those lies about God and ourselves, and when we hit that rock bottom, we stop sharing God's truth with others. Game over. Satan "1", us "0".

As always, however, when we are feeling unsure, God's word is there to pick us up. In Proverbs 23:18, King Solomon writes, "There is surely a future hope for you, and your hope will not be cut off." Faith is believing God's word, even if we can't see it right away. For example, if you hold this target up in front of you, and your partner hits that target, you know it will protect your body. You don't have to question that it will protect you every time your partner hits it, because you know that it has protected you every time in the past. It is the same with God's word. If we are going to stop those fiery arrows, we have to have faith in God and believe as said in 1 John 4:4: "…the one who is in you is greater than the one who is in the world."

This week, I challenge you all to remember a time that God has come through for you or your family. It is during these times that He has helped us that we need to remember that He is always working in our lives, even if we can't see it all the time.

Use the space below to add your thoughts, experiences, and convictions to make this message more personal for your audience.

Day 45: The Helmet of Salvation

Key Verse(s): Ephesians 6:17
"Take the helmet of salvation and the sword of the Spirit, which is the word of God."

*****Keep a sparring helmet handy for demonstration today*****

Students, who would feel safe if I sent you into a sparring match without one of these today? What would be the danger in going into battle without a head covering? *(Allow students to answer)*

The truth is, your brain controls your entire body, from telling your heart to pump, telling your lungs to breathe, telling your body to move to block a hit or telling your hand to strike, and so many other functions that we need to survive but don't even realize are going on all the time. Without a properly working brain, we would not be here today, and that alone makes protecting your head from injury a huge priority.

In ancient times, soldiers wore helmets to battle for the very same reason, but in our key verse today, Paul is talking about more than just protection from physical trauma. What else does your brain do? *(Allow students to answer)* It thinks! Is it possible that Paul is talking about protecting ourselves from the wrong kind of thoughts?

Think about this. If I asked you to jump ten feet across the floor, do you think you could do it? If the whole class was yelling, "You can do it!" would you feel good about it? But what if we were saying, "You'll never do it! You can't do it!" How would you feel about it then? Or what if I said that if you failed, you would have to do 100 push-ups? That might just mess with your head a little bit, wouldn't it? You might have those negative thoughts running around, and that would affect your attitude and abilities.

Everything that we think in our minds affects us in some way. And dwelling on sinful thoughts, lies from the enemy (even if it comes from other people's mouths), or even anxiety and worry from ourselves can render us powerless when engaging the enemy in battle. If we protect our bodies, shouldn't we protect our minds as well? Absolutely! God especially knows the debilitating effects of negative thinking, and in Philippians 4:8, Paul writes: "Finally, brothers and sisters, whatever is true, whatever is noble, whatever is right, whatever is pure, whatever is lovely, whatever is admirable – if anything is excellent or praiseworthy – think about such things."

The other piece to this puzzle is a question: What are you allowing in the space between your ears? Are you watching movies that cause you to have negative or sinful thoughts? Do you listen to music with foul language? Are you spending time with people who speak negatively all the time or constantly gossip about others? If so, you aren't wearing that helmet properly, and you are unprotected!

This week, assess what thoughts you are allowing into your mind. If you catch yourself thinking something you know isn't right, remember this sparring helmet and seek to fill your mind with only good things.

Use the space below to add your thoughts, experiences, and convictions to make this message more personal for your audience.

Day 46: The Sword of the Spirit

Key Verse(s): Ephesians 6:17
"Take the helmet of salvation and the sword of the Spirit, which is the word of God."

*****Instructors, if you have weapons training in your school, consider having a katana, bo staff, or other similar weapon for demonstration today during mat time.*****

If I were to go into battle empty handed, how do you think I would feel about going up against someone else? What if I were to go into battle with a weapon? *(If you have a weapon to demonstrate, do so now and demonstrate a couple of techniques with it)* You see, the past few weeks, we have been talking about defensive pieces of armor, but today, we have something that is offensive. Does anyone know what that means? Offensive means you are making a physical attack on someone, and though you technically could defend yourself with some weapons, they are primarily used to inflict damage to the other person.

Let's take a look at today's key verse again. What does it say the sword of the Spirit is? *(Allow students to answer)* It is the word of God! Is a sword any good if it is dull? Sure, it can still be of some use, but let's see just how sharp the sword of the spirit is. Hebrews 4:12 tells us that it is "alive and active, sharper than any double-edged sword." Who would feel more comfortable going into battle with one of those?

You might be asking how one can win a battle with the Word of God. Let's look through scripture and find a classic story about Jesus using that same sword against Satan. In the book of Matthew, chapter 4, we find Jesus weak and hungry in the desert, having been fasting for 40 days. Satan came to Him and tempted Him to turn some stones into bread. Jesus replied in verse 4: "It is written: 'Man shall not live on bread alone, but on every word that comes from the mouth of God.'" Jesus "1", Satan "0". Also, note that the enemy approached Jesus when he thought He was at His weakest. Satan is quite the opportunist!

That is another reminder for us to never let our guard down!

Afterwards, Satan took Jesus to the highest point of the temple in Jerusalem and tempted Him to throw Himself down, trusting in God's protection. Again, we see a flash of that sword as Jesus replies in verse 7: "It is also written: 'Do not put the Lord your God to the test.'" Jesus "2", Satan "0".

Satan tries one last time to win Jesus over, this time appealing to pride. He offers Jesus all of the kingdoms of the world if He would only bow down and worship him.

Are you thinking what I'm thinking? Why would Jesus be interested in a dying world when He has seen the splendor of Heaven? Jesus answers in verse 10: "Away from me, Satan! For it is written: 'Worship the Lord your God, and serve him only.'" Jesus "3", Satan "0". This ends the match.

Did you see how each time, Jesus used the literal Word of God to fight against the evil one? That's what it looks like to have a sword of the spirit.

This week, I challenge you to sharpen your swords of the spirit. Get in the word and try to commit at least one Bible verse to memory. Remember, the more verses you have, the more effective your offensive attacks will be.

Use the space below to add your thoughts, experiences, and convictions to make this message more personal for your audience.

Day 47: The Good Fight

Key Verse(s): 2 Timothy 4:7
"I have fought the good fight, I have finished the race, I have kept the faith."

How many of you like earning your way up the belt ranks as you train in class each week? There is something special about earning a new color belt and having the added responsibility of more information, training, and requirements that go along with it. What are your goals for this class? Is it to make it to purple belt? How about blue belt? Brown belt is an admirable goal (and it comes with the nice perk of _____). How many of you are going for the gold in trying to attain your black belt one day? That is quite an honor, and one you will have to work harder for than you have likely worked for anything else in your life to earn it.

For those of you who raised your hand that last time, what are your plans after you earn your black belt? Is that the end-goal for you? Does it even work that way?

The truth is, your 1st dan black belt is just the beginning. It proves to everyone that you have mastered the basics, but it says nothing of what you can do if you continue your training. Will you invest more time into your own training, or will you aspire to become a teacher yourself? Are you willing to invest in other people's goals and aspirations?

Those are some serious questions that I doubt many of you have even considered so far. But they are worthy of serious contemplation.

In today's verse, Paul is writing to Timothy to let him know that he is suffering, near the end of his life, and chained like a criminal, but despite this fact, he wants Timothy to remind everyone that God's word cannot be chained. He may be at the end of his earthly life, but the word of God will never have an end. What most people would consider Paul's end (or possibly what Paul has to say about God's word) is really just taking another form. There never really is an end, and as Isaiah 55:11 reminds us, "...so is my word that goes out from my mouth: It will not return to me empty, but will accomplish what I desire and achieve the purpose for which I sent it."

Rare is the person who accomplishes what they set out to do, but rarer still is the one who continues on once they have achieved that perceived finish line. If your goal is to read the Bible, start it again once you finish it. If you strive to bring five people to Jesus, keep working at it after those five. If God is calling you to compose a song, write a book, or build a building for Him, keep them coming once you've hit that goal.

And whether or not your goal is that black belt, aim to continue on long after you've received it. For all things that you "go the extra mile" in, the rewards are well worth it.

Use the space below to add your thoughts, experiences, and convictions to make this message more personal for your audience.

_____

_____

_____

_____

_____

_____

_____

_____

_____

_____

_____

_____

_____

_____

_____

_____

Day 48: Looking Beyond Ourselves

Key Verse(s): Hebrews 11:1
"Now faith is confidence in what we hope for and assurance about what we do not see."

Students, how would you each feel if I told you that you would be testing tomorrow? For some of you who just earned your current rank, that would probably be a scary thought, but for others who are nearing your next test requirements, it might be less scary. Even so, there might still be some hesitation on your part. Why would that be? Would you feel as if you were not prepared? For some of you, that would be an accurate statement. Maybe you would want a few more practice sessions before you are put on the spot? The good news is that I wouldn't do that to you because truthfully, the majority of you would not be ready to undertake that task on such a short notice. I do hope, though, that when I tell all of you that it is time to test, that you have faith in my experience and judgement, both in the martial arts and in your individual abilities to adequately make that call.

You see, testing often requires faith in something other than your own feelings; it takes faith in the one who brings the opportunity to you. Sometimes, focusing on your faith in the other person takes some of the anxiety out of trying to trust yourself.

The Bible is *full* of people who did amazing things, not because they thought they could do it themselves, but because God told them to, and they trusted Him. What would have happened if Noah didn't trust God when He told him to build a huge ark for water that would be pouring down from the sky? (Remember, no one had seen rain up until that point.) What if Sarah or Elizabeth didn't have faith that God would give them a child, even though they were past the child-bearing age? What if Moses did not have faith that he could free the Israelites from their position of slavery in Egypt? (Granted, he was worried until God told him that Aaron would help him, but nonetheless, he still carried out the plans). Because of Moses' faith, all of the Israelites, in turn, saw great signs and wonders leading up to their departure from Egypt that only solidified their faith as well. (How could someone not have faith after seeing the Red Sea part and make way for them?)

Do you all remember the story of Gideon? Imagine leading an army into battle and having God tell you to cut your army down not just once, but twice, until only 300 remained? All of these people and so many others relied on the knowledge of the One who had a higher perspective than they did, and because of their acts of faith, they made history. Now their stories serve as reminders for all of us that it is not always in ourselves that we should be placing our faith.

Jeremiah 17:9 reminds us, "The heart is deceitful above all things and beyond cure." Furthermore, John 14:1 encourages, "Do not let your heart be troubled. You believe in God…"

This week, I challenge you all to reassess where you place your faith. Is it in worldly things, legalistic ideas, or even your expectations? Let's strive to have faith in the One who truly sees all things past, present, and to come as He stated many times in the New Testament, "Your faith has healed you."

Use the space below to add your thoughts, experiences, and convictions to make this message more personal for your audience.

Day 49: Fruitful or Not?

Key Verse(s): Psalm 119:37
"Turn my eyes away from worthless things; preserve my life according to your word."

Having done many tournaments since I was a teenager, there was one thing I just couldn't grasp. How can people base the validity of their entire martial arts training solely by the number of trophies they had on display in their rooms at home? Tournaments are not a bad thing, and in fact, they do have many benefits to your martial arts training. But it never seemed right (or logical) to me that every weekend should be dedicated to them, or that a true, talented martial artist is one that can beat countless others in a ring just to earn the title of "national champion." Please understand, having titles and tournament experience is not the problem; the issue actually goes much deeper.

Today's key verse reminds us that we have fruitful deeds and unfruitful ones, and tournaments aren't good or bad, per say, it's how we treat them. Are we using tournaments (or other sport gatherings) as a way to encourage others, make new friends, share Truth, or ask for prayer? Or are they filling an insatiable desire for worldly approval, putting ourselves in the limelight, or receiving reverence from others? This may be a convicting question for you all: Are these seemingly innocent gatherings filling your time with thoughts of "me me me?" If so, tread lightly, for this is a form of self-worship.

In all things, we should be asking if we are seeking to honor ourselves or to honor God. Today's key verse tells us that we should not be investing in things that are deemed worthless; rather, we should be honoring God with our time. We are reminded of this in the book of Revelation, beginning in Chapter 2, as Paul was writing letters to the seven churches. For the majority of them, there were some major changes that needed to happen in their hearts. Let's take a quick look at what these churches needed to work on:

- Ephesus had forsaken their first love (Jesus)
- Smyrna was warned that they would suffer slander and persecution
- Pergamum needed repentance
- Thyatira had a false prophetess (idol)
- Sardis had "fallen asleep" (unfinished deeds)
- Philadelphia kept Jesus' commands and patiently endured (good job Philadelphia!)
- Laodicea had lukewarm faith (remember what God says about that?)

This week, I challenge you to look not only at where you spend the majority of your time, but also your intentions in doing so. Ultimately, we should follow in the way of Jesus, who in all things, first sought God's approval rather than that of the crowds. As Psalm 19:14 reminds us, "May these words of my mouth and this meditation of my heart be pleasing in your sight, Lord, my Rock and my Redeemer."

Use the space below to add your thoughts, experiences, and convictions to make this message more personal for your audience.

Day 50: Birds of the Sky

Key Verse(s): Genesis 1:20
"And God said, 'Let the water teem with living creatures, and let birds fly above the earth across the vault of the sky.'"

The presence of birds in nearly every area of the world offers a unique perspective with which to see. Regardless of whether the birds can actually fly or not, we cannot dispute that these magnificent creatures have found their way into the history of countless countries via folklore, artwork, superstitions, spiritual beliefs, and ways of life.

In China, the crane is considered a messenger from heaven and because of this, is associated with longevity. It is also representative of one of the five traditional styles of Ng Ying Kung Fu, each of which incorporates attributes of these animals into their martial art. This can include stances, battle cries, and movement mannerisms. In the case of the crane, due to this bird's physical build, this "school" focuses on a gentle approach to their style.

In Japan, roosters are deemed sacred, for they are attributed with the power of chasing away the dark of the night with their cry at dawn. Because of their place in Japanese lore, they are given free reign, even in the famous Shinto Temples, located all over Japan.

In the Bible, however, we see the birds portrayed in various ways. One way is found in the book of Genesis, chapter 8, verse 6 when Noah releases a raven from the ark to see if the waters had receded enough for him and his family to return to land again. As stated in verse 7, "…it kept flying back and forth until the water had dried up from the earth." Interestingly, ravens are incredibly adaptable birds and can survive on plant life, as well as dead animals. For this reason, the raven likely preferred being out of the boat, for it could find food in the likely abundance of animal carcasses and rest on the water surface for hours at a time before flying again. It was when Noah sent out the dove that he got a more accurate idea of how safe the landscape was, for doves will not stay where there is no land to rest on. The "all clear" is given in verse 11 where we read,

"When the dove returned to him in the evening, there in its beak was a freshly plucked olive leaf! Then Noah knew that the water had receded from the earth."

In Matthew 24:28, we see the vulture as a sign of omen: "Wherever there is a carcass, there the vultures will gather." Yet in Isaiah 40:31, we see a bird used as a sign of hope: "…but those who hope in the Lord will renew their strength. They will soar on wings like eagles…"

Birds are also used to portray God's providence and care in the Bible. In Luke 12:24, we read, "Consider the ravens: They do not sow or reap, they have no storeroom or barn; yet God feeds them. And how much more valuable you are than birds!" Furthermore, in Matthew 10:29, we see, "Are not two sparrows sold for a penny? Yet not one of them will fall to the ground outside your Father's care."

Through all these references, however, we see the dove consistently portrayed as the presence of the Holy Spirit. In Matthew 3:16, we read, "As soon as Jesus was baptized, he went out of the water. At that moment heaven was opened, and he saw the Spirit of God descending like a dove and alighting on him."

Of all the birds in the Bible, the dove is the one that carries special meaning as a symbol of God's redemption and presence. This week's challenge is to do a bit of bird watching to see if you can see how these special animals further glorify our Creator.

Use the space below to add your thoughts, experiences, and convictions to make this message more personal for your audience.

Day 51: Sacred Space

Key Verse(s): Exodus 3:5
"'Do not come any closer,' God said. 'Take off your sandals, for the place where you are standing is holy ground.'"

Raise your hands if you know why we take our shoes off during our martial arts classes? Did you know that this is actually a deeply rooted cultural expectation that originates in Japan? Does anyone know why we do this?

In this room, we have hard flooring, but in ancient Japan, that was not the case. Japanese homes initially had a wood flooring, but on top there would be tatami mats, which are very thin and made with woven straw so they could be rolled up and moved. Typically, the mats were used for sitting or sleeping on, but by the 1500's, tatami flooring was being used throughout the entire home. The versatility and beauty of this flooring made them incredibly popular, but they had a major drawback. Shoes would damage this flooring over time. So, the custom of removing one's shoes before entering was not just one of cleanliness, but also to preserve the flooring. Think about it this way: If you were invited to a friend's house for a meal, would you thank them by knocking holes in their walls? Of course not!

Today's key verse references when Moses was tending his sheep in Midian. As he came to Mount Horeb, he came upon a bush that was on fire, yet not burning up. As he moved closer to inspect the bush, he heard God's voice telling him to remove his shoes, for he was on holy ground. The idea of removing one's shoes out of respect for the sacredness or cleanliness of the space was not foreign by any means.

We also see this custom of removing one's shoes throughout Bible history and tradition. For example, shoes are typically not worn in the homes of those who practice Judaism (but that's also the case with many other faiths). In addition, shoes are forbidden for priests and those of Aaronic descent when priestly blessings are given.

In the case of leather shoes, customary practice also involves removing them before approaching a holy person's grave, (today's key verse in action), during an annual fast day called Tisha B'Av, during Yom Kippur, or during the seven days of mourning after losing a loved one. In the case of the latter, it is customary in Jewish practice to put a pebble or small amount of dirt into their shoes if they have to go out to run errands or go to a Synagogue during this time.

What's important to know about these customs is that we may not understand the depth of them or practice them as Christians, but our faith is rooted in the laws and customs of God's chosen people. Furthermore, to understand the customs that Jesus experienced while growing up only gives us more insight into the character and mannerisms of our Savior, which is of upmost importance if we want to try to live our lives in a manner that brings Him glory.

This week, if you don't already have a rule about leaving your shoes by the front door, practice doing so. Try to remember not just the idea that you are keeping your floors clean, but that you are also recognizing your home as a sacred space in a dark world.

Use the space below to add your thoughts, experiences, and convictions to make this message more personal for your audience.

Day 52: Bond Servanthood

Key Verse(s): Luke 9:23
"Then he said to them all: 'Whoever wants to be my disciple must deny themselves and take up their cross daily and follow me.'"

Let's go back in time to the late 1300's AD during the Koryo dynasty and learn a little bit about a man named Chong Mong-Chu. This man was a famous diplomat, politician, and poet that was also known by his pseudonym "Po Un", after which a Korean kata was created to commemorate him and his contribution to Korean literature. His poem, "I would not serve another master though I might be crucified a hundred times' is well known to all Koreans and is an amazing example of humility, loyalty, and servanthood. What is interesting to note is that his "master" was the King (King U), and that Chong Mong-Chu was assassinated for being a Koryo loyalist during a time of political upheaval.

Servanthood was not a new concept in the 1300's, and we see many cases in the Bible where people were sold or traded into slavery or kidnapped for that same purpose. Earlier this year, we even talked about Joseph and how his brothers had kidnapped him and sold him as a slave.

Fast forward to the New Testament, and we see many instances where Jesus' disciples referred to themselves as "bond servants", and I want us to take a closer look at this tradition that goes back to Old Testament Times. In Deuteronomy 15, we learn that Hebrew men or women could sell themselves as slaves for a period of six years, but that during the seventh year, they were to be released. In verse 16, we see another option they had available to them once they were freed: "But if your servant says to you, 'I do not want to leave you,' because he loves you and your family and is well off with you, then take an awl and push it through his earlobe into the door, and he will become your servant for life."

In these verses, we see some interesting concepts:

- A servant can choose to live with and continue to serve their master, but it is a lifelong commitment.
- Becoming a bond servant entails having your ear pierced as part of the pledge.
- Becoming a bond servant is a show of the servant's love for their master, rather than a forced relationship.

Let's look at the first point from the lens of others who have identified as "slaves of" or "bond servants of" Christ and also died in their loyalty to the King of Kings. James and Jude were both half-brothers of Jesus and considered themselves believers (even if the majority of the convincing came after Jesus' resurrection). In addition, Paul expounded on the concept of servanthood in Romans 6:16, "'Don't you know that when you offer yourselves to someone as obedient slaves, you are slaves of the one you obey – whether you are slaves to sin, which leads to death, or to obedience, which leads to righteousness?'"

On the second point, we see an act that reflects a concept that we have discussed before in the Passover celebration, ultimately pointing to Jesus' crucifixion. Having an ear pierced with an awl on a door (or a doorpost) is a reminder of Jesus' commitment to us via the shedding of blood upon a wooden door or frame that also leaves a piercing and scar. In addition, we see in John 13 that Jesus further exemplified the concept of servanthood by washing the feet of His disciples the night before His death.

Finally, we are not forced to accept Jesus into our hearts. God gives us free will to decide for ourselves, as stated in today's key verse. As mentioned above, this is a decision that must be made out of love and respect for the master, not out of fear, coercion, or manipulation. God loves us SO much that He gives us the ultimate choice.

This week, I challenge each of you to consider what being a bond servant to Christ really means in your lives.

Use the space below to add your thoughts, experiences, and convictions to make this message more personal for your audience.

Day 53: Ceaseless

Key Verse(s): 1 Thessalonians 5:16
"Rejoice always, pray continually, give thanks in all circumstances; for this is God's will for you in Christ Jesus."

Students, we have been on an incredible journey throughout this book, challenging ourselves spiritually and learning more about not only our own faith, but how the customs of God's chosen people have set the patterns in Old Testament times for what we have seen, or can expect to see, in the New Testament times. I want to finish our Mat Time book with an encouragement found in our key verse today. *(Reread verse)*

What exactly does it mean to rejoice always? As believers in Christ, we know that hard times will come that require us to have spiritual fortitude. During these times, will we choose to praise the Lord, regardless of the season, or will we wallow in "why me's?" Will we choose to see the miracle of each day given to us by God, or will we allow the world to wear us down, little by little, until we fall into a pattern of trying to fill a God-hole with earthly things, wants, and desires? Will we forget all that we have learned, or will we always remember that we serve a God of miracles?

One pattern we've learned about the frailty of humankind is that we tend to become complacent and forget the mighty things that have been done for us. Because of this, I highly encourage all of you to read your Bibles so that you can take a stand when the enemy strikes. As Psalm 119:11-16 says, "I have hidden your word in my heart that I might not sin against you. Praise be to you, Lord; teach me your decrees. With my lips I recount all the laws that come from your mouth. I rejoice in following your statues as one rejoices in great riches. I meditate on your precepts and consider your ways. I delight in your decrees; I will not neglect your word."

In addition, I encourage you all to continue talking to the Lord each day through prayer. Do you remember when we talked about the armor of God? There was a verse regarding the sword of the spirit that we didn't discuss then, because I wanted to save it for today. Ephesians 6:18 states, "And pray in the

Spirit on all occasions with all kinds of prayers and requests. With this in mind, be alert and always keep on praying for all the Lord's people." Despite what we may think (or the enemy tries to tell us), not one of our prayers goes unheard. We serve a God that cares so much about us that He humbled Himself to becoming an earthly sacrifice out of *love*.

Finally, we are called to give thanks. If you woke up this morning, have breath in your lungs, or found beauty in God's creation outside, we are called to give thanks. If you have a family that loves you, friends who are loyal, or food on your table, you should express your gratitude. Even if you are having a bad day or going through a hard time, we must first give praise and thanks, for God deserves all the honor.

It is my hope and prayer that this book has served to test you in your faith, challenged you in ways that you may not have been challenged before, and helped you to grow in your understanding of our Lord Jesus. But what will you *do* with this knowledge? It is my desire that one day, we will all hear in the words of Jesus himself, "Well done, good and faithful servant!"

Use the space below to add your thoughts, experiences, and convictions to make this message more personal for your audience.

Bibliographic References

Kasdan, Barney. *God's Appointed Customs – A Messianic Jewish Guide to the Biblical Lifecycle and Lifestyle.* Lederer Books, 1996.

Kasdan, Barney. *God's Appointed Times – A Practical Guide for Understanding and Celebrating the Biblical Holidays.* Lederer Books, 2007.

Larson, Rick. "*The Star of Bethlehem*", 2023, https://www.bethlehemstar.com.

About The Author

Ginny Aversa Tyler is a wife and mother of four children. She is the owner and founder of DMD Tae Kwon Do, a Christian martial arts school near McKinney, Texas. (www.dmdtaekwondo.com)

Inspired by the endless lessons both God's Word and the martial arts have to offer, Ginny has written multiple publications so that others can tie their love of the martial arts to the lifelong guidance our Heavenly Father offers in a tangible way for their classrooms, students, and families.

Ginny's passion for teaching, not just her own children and students, is the basis for her books, through which she wishes to inspire children and instructors all over the world to seek Biblical truths outside the walls of their home, school, and martial arts classes.

Other Titles by Ginny Tyler

Kingdom Kicks Series:

A Lesson On Perseverance
A Lesson On Humility
A Lesson On Self-Control
A Lesson On Courtesy
A Lesson On Indomitable Spirit
A Lesson On Integrity
A Lesson On Obedience
A Lesson On Strength
Kingdom Kicks Coloring Book
Lessons From The Mat
A Lesson On Wisdom

(Bonus materials for Kingdom Kicks series
available on www.dmdtaekwondo.com)

Under The Door

Mat Time
*Devotions to Enrich Your Martial Arts
Classes*

All Books Available on Amazon!

.

www.ingramcontent.com/pod-product-compliance
Lightning Source LLC
Chambersburg PA
CBHW071344090426
42738CB00012B/3012